Scribe Publications

GREEK PILGRIMAGE

AF864152

For Eva

GREEK PILGRIMAGE

IN SEARCH OF THE FOUNDATIONS OF THE WEST

JOHN CARROLL

SCRIBE
Melbourne

Scribe Publications Pty Ltd
PO Box 523
Carlton North, Victoria, Australia 3054
Email: info@scribepub.com.au

First published by Scribe 2010

Copyright © John Carroll 2010

All rights reserved. Without limiting the rights under copyright reserved above, no part of this publication may be reproduced, stored in or introduced into a retrieval system, or transmitted, in any form or by any means (electronic, mechanical, photocopying, recording or otherwise) without the prior written permission of the publishers of this book.

Typeset in 11.25/16pt Garamond Premier Pro by the publishers

Printed and bound in China

All photographs are by the author unless credited otherwise.

National Library of Australia
Cataloguing-in-Publication data

Carroll, John, 1944-

Greek Pilgrimage: in search of the foundations of the West

9781921640742 (pbk.)

1. Greece–Description and travel. 2. Greece–History.

914.9504

www.scribepublications.com.au

CONTENTS

KENTRIKI MAKEDONIA
DYTIKI MAKEDONIA
THESSALIA
CHALKIDIKI
AGION OROS
A E G E A N
G R E E C E
VOREIO AIGA
Thessaloniki
Larisa
Volos
Kavala
Thermaikos Kolpos
Kolpos Kassandras
Kolpos Agiou Orous
Pagasitikos Kolpos
Thrakiko Pelagos
Thasos
Voreioi Sporades
Skiathos
Skopelos
Alonnisos
Skyros
Agios Efstratios
Olympos
PELLA
IMATHIA
PIERIA
KOZANI
GREVENA
FLORINA
KASTORIA
TRIKALA
KARDITSA
LARISA
MAGNYSIA
EVRYTANIA
ARTA
FTHIOTIS
Lake Prespa
Notia Pindos

E A
EVVOIA
S T E R E A E L L A S
FOKIS
VOIOTIA
AKARNANIA
ATHINA
(Athens)
Peiraias
Peristerio
Chalandri
ATTIKI
KORINTHIA
ARGOLIS
ARKADIA
ACHAIA
ILIA
MESSINIA
LAKONIA
PELOPONNISOS
Patra
Korinthiakos Kolpos
Saronikos Kolpos
Argolikos Kolpos
Lakonikos Kolpos
Messiniakos Kolpos
Kyparissiakos Kolpos
Patraikos Kolpos
Kolpos Petalion
M I R T O Ö
P E L A G O S
K Y K L A D E S
KYKLADES
(CYCLADES)
N O T I O A I G
Krytiko Pelagos
Andros
Tinos
Syros
Gyaros
Kea
Kythnos
Serifos
Sifnos
Milos
Kimolos
Paros
Antiparos
Sikinos
Folegandros
Antimilos
Aigina
Salamina
Ydra
Spetses
N

THE PARTHENON

PREFACE

In this book, I travel Greece, visiting the ancient sites. My aim is to survey what remains today — the ruins, the vitality, and the aura. A magic or enchantment endures, one that has something to do with the Western genesis, and the fact that our pre-eminent ancestors inhabited these places. I go on to probe the meaning in this for us, and how it is that the ruins still seem so alive, in spite of their obvious decrepitude.

This book is, therefore, a meditation on classical Greece, on its great sites, monuments, and works. It explores their pivotal role in the foundation of the modern world. We who are born into the West are all Greeks.

The ancient Greeks invite us to think about who we are, and the best ways to organise ourselves, to build institutions, and to make our cities beautiful. They inculcate a sceptical orientation to ourselves and the world we inhabit, questioning the meaning. They constantly ask what the good life is. They introduce us to democracy and to sport, to mathematics and to philosophy, and to tragic drama and to music. From Homer onwards, they live in intimate proximity to Nature, finding inspiration in its majesty and power.

In Greece, our metaphysical perspective was set. We were introduced to the *mystery* — an abiding sense that there is a deep secret, one which somehow holds the key to the big questions about life. The travels recorded in this book will be accompanied by some of the classical stories, ones which have been retold for generation upon generation, over the last two-and-a-half thousand years. They include stories of the hero; of the life path as a journey of homecoming; of binding fate; of human acts that transcend the earthly, gaining a divine quality; of the ever-present *daimonic*; of the powers of the feminine; and of the quest in search of the essence of being.

With us throughout this journey will be the challenge of 'culture'. I mean the question of what we should do, who we might be, and how we can understand ourselves, so as to rise above our base biological condition of being like animals, born to eat, grow, breed, and die. Without authoritative culture we are slaves to necessity. We today have lost a convincing language through which we can explore the possibility of higher meaning. Classical Greek culture moved across precisely this territory with a virtuosity and sureness of instinct. Here was the core of its genius.

This is also a sort of travel book, which is designed to serve as a guide for the modern traveller to Greece. I have recommended two alternate itineraries at the end, accompanied by maps and illustrations.

PART I

THE JOURNEY

THE ERECHTHEION

ONE

BORN INTO PILGRIMAGE

The past is a mysterious land that pipes an alluring tune. By night, we dream; by day, we sleepwalk along our life-path; and, all the while, our inner ear strains to pick up a distant, faint rhythm from a long time ago, playing somewhere beyond.

It may be the song of the Sirens serenading the long-voyaging Odysseus. If he were to act on what he hears, bound to the mast of his ship as he is, his rowers' ears sealed with wax; if he were free to follow what rouses him to an ecstatic swoon, his journey would be dashed to pieces on a rocky shore. By all means listen, his story instructs us, but don't sail too close to the enchantment! Or, it may be the voice of the goddess Athena that is heard, as she sings the foundation story in Western culture, the *Iliad*, through the voice of the poet Homer. Her story tells of the wonder and the tragedy, of what it was like, once upon a time, to live in the age of heroes. Her song implies that, ever since, things have been lesser, but that we lesser mortals may aspire to rise above our ordinariness.

Of course, it is not just any past that breathes a mystery call.

Is it that we are after some metaphysical homecoming — or *nostos*, as it is named in Greek by Homer in his second work, the *Odyssey*? Nostalgia is a perpetual longing for some idyllic past, a feeling something akin to mellow grief over distant loss. And, indeed, the English word 'nostalgia' is a Greek derivative — from *nostos algos* — meaning literally pain for home, or grief, or suffering.

It is as if our perpetual, cursed condition is to have awoken one day after a long sleep to find ourselves in an alien place, removed from our primal home: a home of which we can conjure up no conscious picture, however hard we try; a home that we know only by some sixth sense, and a deep instinctual longing. It is as if, to continue, our other home and its family, the well-known one, the haven in which we grew up, is just a substitute attempt by loving parents to console us for our loss. They, too, those parents, built their nest, a cosy security of sought-for belonging, in an attempt to console themselves for the same loss.

So it is that we are enthralled by origins. We are pitched at birth into a life-long quest to find our primordial spiritual home, the place where it truly began. So we travel, and not only on foot. We travel in our teeming imagination, pressured with fantasies of where it might be better, with whom it might be right. But aren't those particular fantasies mere displacements, substitutes supplying goals that seem more achievable? Where were we in the beginning? How are we to find our way back? How are we to discover the clues that matter?

Even the ultra-rational Socrates had a dream, just before his death, of meeting a stunningly beautiful woman dressed in white robes, who told him that he was about to undertake a three-day voyage to Phthia.[1] The association is with Book 9 of the *Iliad*, in which Achilles anticipates leaving Troy the next day, and taking the three-day voyage back to his beloved home, which is Phthia. Socrates is dreaming, as he departs from life, of joining the legendary hero on a journey to his true home. Wherever that may be, it is far from Athens, the actual place in which Socrates has always lived.

There are more straightforward answers to why we travel, or at least travel to other countries and remote places. There is curiosity — we humans seem to be born with some restlessness of spirit, and a hankering for difference and change. We are curious to see differences of place (both landscape and human settlement), of people, of customs, of food, and, in general, of taste and ethos. A good part of this is to test our own home — suburb, city, and nation, by means of comparison, and with it our own habits, beliefs, and what we think we know.

To go further, we travel in order to find clues about how to live. This may turn into a search for exemplary ancestors — for lessons about what they were like, and how they lived. This blurs into the quest for central truths — which we imagine, if only we could find them, would explain things. It blurs into the quest for the homecoming to where we were in the beginning.

Ambitious travelling over unfamiliar territory involves many petty challenges beyond charting an itinerary: from booking flights, to finding and managing airports; from finding out how to hire cars, to learning unfamiliar highway codes; from locating train and bus timetables, to buying tickets and finding departure points. Then there are the constant decisions that need to be made about where to sleep, where and what to eat, and, above all, what to see, where it is, and when it is open. Much of this process is fraught with tension, with a background worry about all the things that might go wrong — especially the prospect of being stranded in some alien place where one doesn't speak the language.

Travelling is, typically, gruelling and nerve-wracking hard work, a tense ordeal that can turn to nightmare. Why, then, do so many pitch themselves into it, and do so with high expectation and hope? True, travelling is saved, in part, by seeing and experiencing things that are impressive and edifying. There is the grandeur of Cologne Cathedral, the idyllic rural beauty of a Cotswold village, the charm of a Paris café, the gentle warmth of Thai manners.

Once in a while, the traveller is inspired; but, in my experience this does not happen very often. At one level, the traveller may be regularly struck by admiration — nodding the head in acknowledgement that what I am looking at is impressive, recognising that these people do this well. At a quite different level, there is inspiration. A chasm separates the two reactions. Being inspired, one is taken out of oneself: there is a sense of awe; there is the breathtaking feeling that one is in the presence of something that is timeless, and greater than human. For me, this has happened when walking in central Rome (predominantly seventeenth-century Rome); inside Bourges Cathedral, and to a lesser degree inside Amiens and Salisbury Cathedrals; at the north end of the Sea of Galilee; in the Alhambra in Granada; and, I should say, in Australia, along some coastlines and on Mt Buffalo. The experience is more common in engagement with rare works of art, literature, music, and film — but that is a different story.

Greece has been like no other place. There, I have found frequent inspiration. Certainly, this sensation has been linked to specific sites. But there is also something cumulative, an aura that is pan-Hellenic, to use the ancient term. It may be to do with some spirit of the place, anchored in half-a-dozen specially charged locations.

Here I have never felt let down. It is as if that tune of eternal homecoming pipes through this land. Instinctively, I respond. Indeed, I am writing this book in an attempt to fathom what is going on, in search of those things that, in Shakespeare's words in his farewell play, 'doth suffer a sea-change into something rich and strange'. I can only hope that my perplexity is a fertile one.

I have always been drawn to this journey. On my first visit to Europe from Australia, aged twenty-two, I insisted on travelling by Greek ship, rather than flying, so that my first sight of land should be Piraeus, the port of Athens.

What follows is then both a personal story and a reflection on the nature of culture — what we think we know and value. I am representative, responding in more than a subjective way, for I carry within me the general Western disposition. I carry within the same cultural baggage as everyone who has been born into the modern West.

The heritage from ancient Greece, and especially Athens, directly to us is overwhelming. Although elusive to chart in its entirety, it includes some more obvious traditions. There is a fundamental individualism — a belief in a human dignity centred on individuals being free and independent. This feeds into the democratic political mode. There is a spirit of free enquiry, and a curiosity about the world in which we live, including about our own natures as human beings, the way our communities function, the plants and other creatures that inhabit the earth, and the constitution of that earth, other planets, and the universe. This comes with a rugged scepticism, a need to question inherited belief and custom, and to reflect on life. Our scientific tradition derives from here; this is illustrated by our mathematics continuing to use Greek symbols, and our medicine, Greek words. There is, further, the belief that the good life needs to be surrounded by beauty: elegant buildings and gardens; fine works of art; graceful and brilliant performances in sport, drama, and public speech; and courteous etiquette among people.

In my case, there have been particular influences. My mother was a passionate lover of things Greek — especially early-Greek sculpture. I discovered Plato when I was sixteen, and would try to engage a few of my schoolmates in discussion of Platonic ideas. (They didn't always roll their eyes.) Later, my principal academic interest gelled: the nature of culture — that is, the stories and images through which people try to understand their lives, and to find meaning in what they do. The three most significant influences on me outside classical Greece itself have been the German philosopher Friedrich Nietzsche, and especially his first book, *The Birth of Tragedy*, which is itself inspired by ancient Greece; the neo-classical painter Nicolas Poussin; and, in later years, Mark's Life of Jesus, with its own deep affinity with Greek tragedy.

I can give rational explanations for why I am drawn to Greece — I have just done so — but the reality is more mysterious. I am somehow outside the realm of the normal here. What I shall try to evoke in what is to follow is not the typical travelling experience, even at its best.

Illustrious others have passed here before. This is a well-travelled road. There was Alexander the Great, sleeping every night with a copy of the *Iliad* under his pillow, as he restlessly conquered distant regions, from the Danube in the north, to Egypt in the south, and India in the far east — building Greek cities wherever he went based on the Athenian ideal, as taught him by his personal tutor, Aristotle. There was Plutarch, once priest of Apollo at Delphi, reflecting timelessly in his *Lives* on the nature of character and power. There were the Lords Elgin and Byron. There was Thomas Arnold, through his school, Rugby, establishing the educational ideal that governed the English Public Schools; Arnold became the inspiration for the founder of the modern Olympics, Baron Pierre de Coubertin. The universities of Oxford and Cambridge designed their original curriculum on a Greek model. In Germany, there was a procession of Hellenophile poets and philosophers — Winckelmann, Goethe, Hölderlin, Nietzsche, and Heidegger. And in the Renaissance Florence of Lorenzo de Medici, what was being reborn were classical ideals, led by neo-Platonic philosophy. Even the four writers of the Life of Jesus chose Greek as the language in which to craft their story. Luke ends his Life with two men on the road to Emmaus: they are joined by Jesus, who is fleeing Jerusalem, heading north-west, in the direction of Athens.

We were born in ancient Greece, we of the West. This is my working hypothesis. There, in ancient Greece, was our *archē*: our foundation, our genesis, the seed out of which our generic self would grow. It made archaeologists of us all, in the quest to know ourselves — not, of course, archaeologists in the narrow sense, limited to old fragments of stone, bronze, and pottery. This has almost become a truism, given that so many have said it, and over so many generations.

It has induced us into eternal returns, home, to Greece. What were, until the twentieth century, mainly journeys of the mind have become increasingly easy to enact on the ground. I made one of these eternal returns in January 2007 — my fifth. Once there, one feels compelled to travel, or more portentously to 'journey', then as now. And, in journeying, we look, and we reflect, in awe of this land where pagan deities still seem to reign. Looking at the country from this perspective makes the Greek Orthodox Church of later, and modern, times seem like some barbarian mollusc clinging on to a benignly indifferent crag.

And, in reflecting on where the goddess sings, to echo Homer's opening line, it struck me, this time, that five sites preside over our collective Greek past. A journey of this type becomes, inevitably, a type of pilgrimage, in search of an elusive sacred source — as it did for Byron,[2] and for many others. As such, it turns into a narrative with its own anchoring climaxes — just like any one of the big stories, which hinge on 'impression points', nodes of concentrated drama, vectors of subtextual intensity. These five sites may map the culture, at least as it continues to resonate today.

There was the Acropolis in Athens, to which I shall turn later, as I will to the second site, Delphi. There was, thirdly, Mt Olympus. On previous visits, I had not realised the degree to which it dominates northern Greece. It can be seen from a great distance from all directions — the more imposing in January for being capped in snow (see p. 188). There is a majestic, timeless grandeur to its presence, a lofty serenity seen through the crisp, blue winter air. One can hardly move in northern Greece, from Larissa in the south, to Thessaloniki in the north-east, without sensing the epic authority of this dozing giant. For the first time, I understood why the ancient Greeks imagined their gods dwelling here.

Fourthly, there was Olympia. Aptly sited in the Peloponnese near the fabled Arcadia, what strikes one first is the contrast with the harshness of most Greek landscapes. Indeed the later European idyll about arcadia as an earthly paradise might well take Olympia as its model — the ancient travel writer Pausanias described his visit in the second century AD with similar touches of lyricism.[3] Founded in a vale where two rivers met, it is lush, green, fertile, and generously treed (see p. 167). Its mood is soft. For the traveller who arrives from Delphi, it is like a descent from the barren, austere, and vaguely intimidating mountain, to enter a pastoral haven. Even the ruins, set on flat land, have a relaxed, park-like quality to them, inducing a desire to stroll casually among them. The stadium echoes with a leisurely informality, surrounded as it is on three sides by gently rising grassed banks, for spectators — tens of thousands of them. This ease must have contrasted with the scorching ferocity of the athletic competition, where glories of Homeric magnitude might be won.

On the other hand, strolling here, one could be anywhere and nowhere — there is no particular logic as to why this particular, if pleasant, stretch of low land should be of significance. It is not near a port, it is not a great intersection of travel or trade, and there is no city nearby. Indeed the choice is odd, unlike Delphi — which is also remote, but whose site is so arresting that it is easy to believe that the god Apollo, in ancient times, as the *Homeric Hymn to Apollo* attests, should have chosen it as the centre of the world, and the site for his Oracle.

The guidebooks entertain us with the story of the Roman emperor Nero, decamping to Olympia for the Games in AD 67, building a villa for himself, and then competing in the chariot race. He insisted that no other competitor have more than four horses, while he had ten. Nero fell during the race, but nevertheless was declared the winner. I am intrigued by the fact of the most powerful man in the world removing himself from mighty Rome to come to this obscure, green, pastured river-land, just in order to declare himself, fraudulently, the winner of a prize. Even this boorish

Roman was in thrall to Greek culture, enchanted by its elusive tune.

The resonances are powerful and strange. Nero prefigures our world, in which the modern Olympics have become by far the most successful global celebration. In terms of the number of participating countries and individuals, the levels of funding it attracts, and the global interest in it, as measured by television ratings, no gathering or event compares with it. The Soccer World Cup runs a very poor second, and no meeting of international leaders ranks on the same scale. The modern Olympics are truly pan-national, in the same way that the ancient games were pan-Hellenic. Global institutions such as the United Nations can only look on in astonishment and envy at the international goodwill that the Olympics manage to inspire every four years.

Our Games, in spite of regular corruption and drug scandals, have succeeded in combining athletics with a higher ideal. In the great performances it ushers forth, there is a kind of secular or pagan transcendence. The Games' founder, Pierre de Coubertin, sought to bring back 'athletic religion' — and he succeeded. Strolling around the ruins of Olympia (as he did in the late nineteenth century), it feels like the ancient mysteries that dwell here are eternally ready to be kindled back to life. The West responds instantly to their charm.

My fifth and final site was Mycenae. Bleak and foreboding, it is set among grey, rocky, inhospitable hillsides: a brutal fortress built crudely from huge boulders. Its pervading mood is dark — seeming to reflect, three thousand years later, the atrocities that happened within. A king served his brother a pie with his own children's cooked remains inside; a queen murdered her husband on his return from a ten-year war; her son took revenge by killing her; and so on. It is of little surprise that Mycenaean civilisation lasted for only two centuries, given a ruling elite with such monstrous proclivities.[4] Yet, it was from this microcosm of human horror that the Greek expedition which attacked Troy was initiated and led, without which we would not have Homer's *Iliad*; nor would we have what is arguably the most profound of the later tragedies, Aeschylus's *Agamemnon*. Mycenae is a counterbalancing opposite to Olympia, a sort of primal warning to unsettle the arcadian idyll. The Mycenaean presence will shadow what is to follow in this book.

As a postscript to my 2007 journey, I would add a sixth site: Delos. Access, today, requires a voyage to the nearby tourist island of Mykonos, followed by a 30-minute trip by small ferry. I finally managed this in spring 2008, having been thwarted in January on an earlier visit because the Delos ferries didn't run in the middle of winter. Delos is the sacred island on which Apollo was born; it is Apollo's island. Along with Delphi, it was the most revered religious site in ancient Greece. Both were pan-Hellenic — not tied to local cults. Delos was the centre of the 'Delian League', in effect the Athenian Empire in its prime. It held the League's treasury, until Perikles moved it to the Acropolis in Athens.

Delos is one of those places that may initially disappoint the modern visitor, yet it leaves an indelible after-image. The ruins are poorly preserved — next to nothing remains from any of Apollo's own temples. Delos lacks the awesome majesty of Delphi, or the breadth of living association of Olympia, where the ruins are more evocative and are complemented by an extensive collection of surviving sculptures housed in the Olympia Museum. While the Delos sanctuary is large and interesting, the spirit that animated it has somehow escaped.

What does remain is a beautiful setting, with an other-worldly mood, as if being here is to be free from the constraints of time and location in life. Apollo's sanctuary is set on gentle, green slopes running down to a quiet inlet, sheltered by a protective semicircle of low hills and knolls. From higher ground to its rear, one looks out across the inlet and the Aegean Sea beyond, to mountains in the distance. Here is an ancient site with an intimate relationship to the sea — a reminder that the classical Greeks were a sea-faring people, and that their imagination was shaped by the rhythms of voyaging, and the risks of crossing the notoriously temperamental Aegean. Delos is a haven from storms at sea, which gives it a timeless, ethereal quality, as a sanctuary from more metaphysical tempests. This quality may explain why it continues to leave a powerful impression.

Travelling through Greece today, what surprises is the vitality of the ancient sites. Alive with their own cast of timeless enchantment, it is as if they haven't changed over the millennia. Somehow, the essences live on. Rationally viewed, a major contributing factor is that the surrounding landscape plays a major role, in all cases except the Acropolis — and even it is only a partial exception. Those landscapes have hardly changed. Eleusis, the site of major ancient religious significance that has lost its surrounds, does fail today to project much classical aura. The resilience of ancient Greece contrasts, to me, with Jerusalem and the Rome of the ancient Romans, neither of which have retained much power to evoke their periods on the grand stage of world history.

Has this miraculous, enduring vitality something to do with the fact that the Western tree that Greece seeded continues to flourish? Or is this just a romantic illusion, a way to redeem the prosaic orders of modern everyday life? Or a fantasy aesthetic–religious culture to populate the disenchanted ruins of the Christian churchyard?

I think not. Our archaeology is more than fantasy, and more than redemptive illusion. Much in our cultural history does become dated. As times change, many works from the past lose their power to speak to us: institutions fall into disrepair, customs die, and rituals are abandoned. Johann Huizinga observed that the hell displayed in the paintings of Hieronymous Bosch is alien to the modern mind.[5] So is the Catholic Last Judgment. We cannot imagine ourselves into this late-medieval cultural universe. The same is true for Renaissance paintings of God as the old man with the long white beard — they leave us coldly detached, and bemused.

This is not the case for the *Iliad*, the *Odyssey*, *Agamemnon*, and *Oedipus the King*, nor indeed for any of the surviving works of classical tragedy or comedy. They still speak to us. So does the Delphic Charioteer and the bronze Zeus of Artemisium. So does classical architecture. So do the social and political analysis of Thucydides, and the philosophies of Plato and Aristotle.

The foundation lives on, in the blood of anybody born into the West. This implies that they must learn to know it, in order to know themselves. For one and all, the *I* that *is*, the still centre of being, the axis of equilibrium in life, needs external screens on which to project itself — lest it waste its days in shy and closeted self-denial. To be drawn out of its lair, so to speak, it must be tempted by its own familiar places. It is the yearning of this *I* that *is* for its primordial home that drives our pilgrimages.

Every person sets out on his or her own Odyssey. At times, as in Chaucer's *Canterbury Tales*, there are others — companion pilgrims — on the same path. The journey is both singular and shared. My invitation to the reader of this book is to accompany me, and to see what happens.

I have opened with actual journeys on the ground, which produced a panorama of six sites governing the ancient-Greek cultural landscape — the Athenian Acropolis, Delphi, Mt Olympus, Olympia, Mycenae, and Delos. I wish now to stand back, in reflection, and to ask how these semi-divine ancestors of ours conceived of the central human problem — what is culture? Where do the sources of meaning lie?

The six sites, taken individually, are not of equal significance. Yet they do contribute to a whole. In dwelling on the logic underpinning that whole, in the hope of coming to understand it, I have reached the view that it is based on three foundation stones. Each is complete, and true to itself. In other words, there are three principal sites where the powerful impulses of the Greek instinct and the Greek spirit came together in one crucible. The fire that then exploded into life generated the field of force out of which the culture, Hellenism, was born. They provide the materials for the whole story.

These three sites are both formative and exemplary. Two of them belong to the physical journey — the Acropolis in Athens, and Delphi. The third, Troy, is a site mainly of the imagination, the setting for what would become the classical Greek Bible — Homer's *Iliad*. The *Iliad* is supplemented by Homer's second work, the *Odyssey*.

Our journey in reflection will begin on the Acropolis in Athens. We shall discover that what is housed there contains the essence of Mycenae: its dark, brooding, malevolent presence. From the Acropolis, we shall travel to Delphi. Delphi, in its turn, includes the spirit of Olympia's 'athletic religion', and does so in an environment in which the predetermining sacred forces are more evident. Third, we move on to Homer, where the real mythic home of the gods is to be found. Whereas many of the threads of legend and custom that contribute to Greek culture predate Homer, it is he who composes the master-work that will form Hellenism and will shape its genius right through to the time of Alexander the Great, and beyond. Mt Olympus, as we know it, was conceived in Homeric Troy. It is those creations of Homer's imagination, furthermore, that breathe spirit into the sacred isle of Delos.

From Homer, I shall go on to reflect on the Greek sense of the sacred, the nature of divinity, and the human experience of transcendence. My focus will be on the goddess Athena and what she represented. Finally, I shall return to the original journey, to its panorama of six sites, and to the heritage question of how our condition today continues to be influenced by ancient Greece, and how it may relate back.

This has been a preamble, a sketching out of the broader scene. Let us now make tracks.

Drawing by M. Korres

TWO

THE ACROPOLIS IN ATHENS

It all began on the Acropolis in Athens. Well, of course, chronologically speaking, it didn't. But for the purposes of my exploration, things begin here. Our journey starts in Athens.

The issue is culture. I mean the Greek view of how we humans can make sense of our lives, find direction, and some sort of vindication. At issue is a theory of culture. Many have trodden this path before me, notably Friedrich Nietzsche. My ambition is to further the way.

The journey opens with two forms: a building and a cluster of six statues. They serve as twin archetypes, principal ones which will help orient what is to follow in this book. On our first morning we stand before the Parthenon and the six Karyatids.

The Acropolis is, in its natural aspect, a single huge crag, a flat-topped hill of rock set in the middle of the metropolis. It has no elegance, grace, or symmetry of form. It is a fitting site for a fortress, but unlikely as the setting for the pre-eminent architectural masterpiece of Western civilisation. Today, the pathway onto it winds up to the Propylaia, a grand, towering, marble-columned entrance hall, flanked by marble buildings — the same route as in the fifth century BC, although people then walked up a long ramp. One emerges from the hall onto the rocky plateau, and it is as if a door has suddenly opened, with the Parthenon right there in front, on slightly higher ground, to the centre-right, drawing the visitor to it.

The Parthenon was built between 447 and 438 BC, to replace its predecessor, which had been destroyed by the Persians in 480 BC. It was built in the Doric style, with Ionic influences, of Pentelic marble. Its explicit purpose was two-fold: to house the gigantic, 10-metre-high statue of Athena commissioned by Perikles, and to serve as a vast, spectacular Treasury housing the wealth of Athens. Pheidias supervised the architects, Iktinos (probably the designer), and Kallikrates (probably the general building contractor)[1]. Pheidias sculpted the statue. While the Parthenon was founded as a temple, dedicated to the goddess Athena, its principal reason for being was to show off the power, wealth, and high cultural eminence of Athens. Athens was proclaiming itself as a cosmopolis, the world city. Perikles had a further, political motive — that of rallying the citizens of Athens, filling them with pride and love of their city, and thereby making them more willing to make sacrifices for its empire.

There is a second building on the Acropolis top, another temple. The Erechtheion was built between 421 and 406 BC — also a part of Perikles' grand plan, but delayed by the Peloponnesian War against Sparta. It is sited on the most sacred part of the Acropolis, where the mythic foundation of Athens occurred. Here, the contest between the gods Athena and Poseidon took place over who could provide the most valuable gift for mortals. Poseidon struck a rock with his trident, and a horse sprang forth. Athena produced an olive tree. (A variant has Poseidon striking a rock, and salt water gushing out, perhaps symbolising Athens' future naval power; this version of the myth is the one represented on the Parthenon.) It was believed that the sacred olive given by Athena grew here. An olive tree grows there today. It is surely a mark of the subtle genius of the ancient Athenians that they should have chosen, counter to plain reason, the olive over the horse. No wonder they charmed the goddess of wisdom!

The Erechtheion likely gets its name from Erechthonius, who may have been the first king of Athens. One myth has it that Hephaistos tried to rape Athena, and during her resistance he ejaculated on her leg. She wiped the semen off with some wool and threw it in disgust on the ground. Erechthonius was born from the fertilised earth, his name being an etymological composite of 'wool' and 'earth'. Athena took in the orphan baby and reared it as her own. Hence, she came to be regarded as the proxy mother of Athens — a virgin mother.[2]

The main temple of the Erechtheion has two parts: one is dedicated to Athena; the other, to Poseidon. Probably it was an attempt to reconcile the two gods. It also has two porches: one on the south, and one on the north. They are the most striking sections of the building today, and it is hard to imagine that this was ever any different.

The southern portico faces up towards the Parthenon. It is dominated by the six Karyatids — larger-than-life sculpted maidens, taking the form of columns that support its roof. Their portico is tacked onto one wall of the temple, which itself is built on lower ground. The northern portico, built on even lower ground,

THE KARYATIDS

and in a different style, stands on the far side, hidden from the Parthenon, close to the edge of the precipitous side of the Acropolis. According to fable, this is where Poseidon's trident struck the rock. It is Poseidon's porch, implying that the southern, Karyatid porch is linked with Athena.

Overall, the Erechtheion is visually incoherent. None of the three components harmonise with each other; their styles clash, as do their three-dimensional massed forms. None of them is of aesthetically pleasing proportions. There is no obvious entrance. One scholar has called the porticos 'asymmetric decorative appendages'.[3] The southern portico leads to a blank wall; it is a doorway to nowhere, although modern scholars have speculated that there would have been a small door leading down steps into the temple.[4] The very lack of symmetry seems to articulate some of the dark pagan mysteries contained within — underground crypts, crevices for sacred snakes, marks in the stone floor where a god's trident struck, and an ancient olivewood idol. That idol, or statue, to accord it more dignity, was later referred to as Athena Polias, and it became the most sacred image on the Acropolis. Women would dress and undress it annually, as if it were some prehistoric fetish — providing it with a newly woven cloak (or *peplos*). Athena Polias was believed to have fallen from the skies.

In all of this, the Erechtheion is opposed and antagonistic to the Parthenon — and we know that each housed its own statue of Athena. The discord is so marked as to seem deliberate, even flagrant — asymmetry contradicting rational order. Moreover, the building as a whole bears no complementariness to the Parthenon. By comparison, the Propylaia was built in alignment and harmony to what it reverently introduced, a rational accompaniment that shows up the violence of the Erechtheion rebellion. Fifth-century

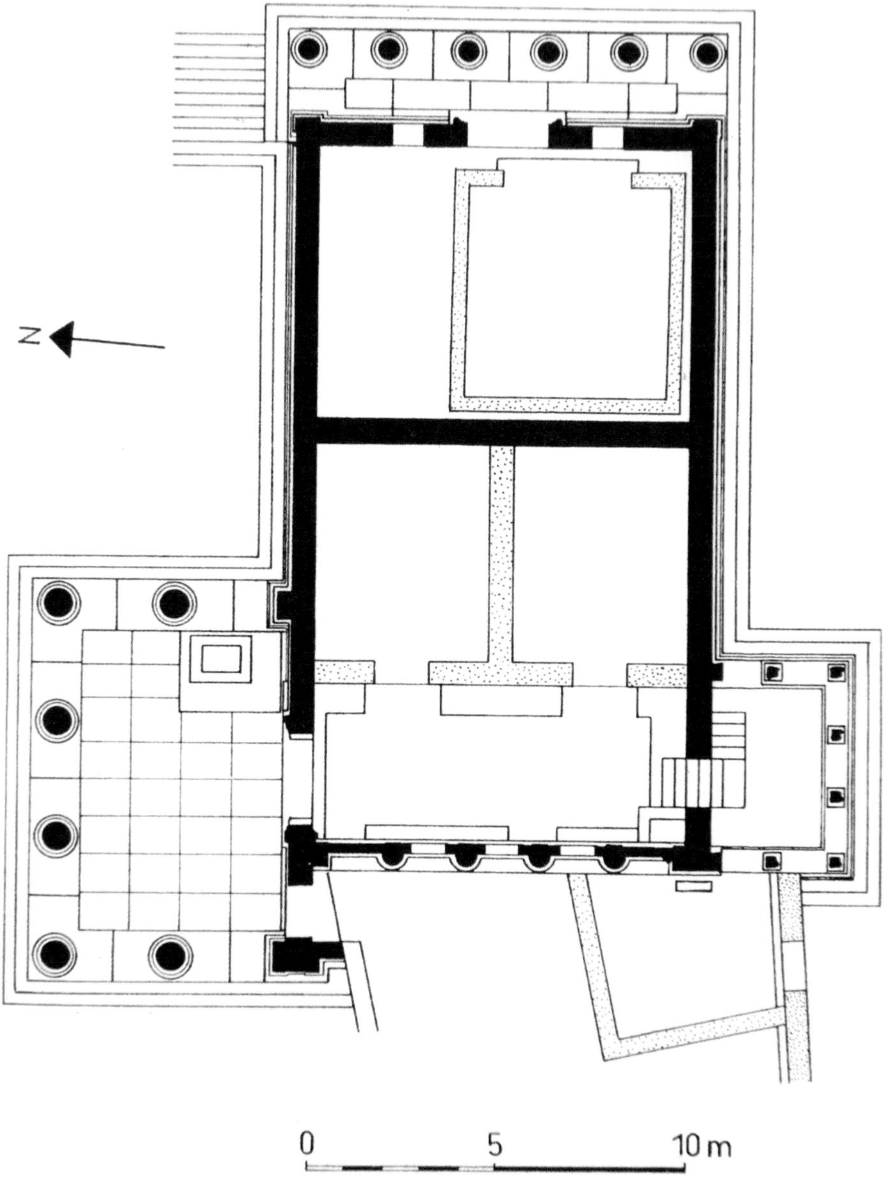

After Goette 2001, Fig. 10

PLAN OF THE ERECHTHEION

Athenians worshipped the primitive statue of Athena Polias, not the huge Athena Parthenos exhibited in the Parthenon.

The six large Karyatid women glower and brood; they are formidable presences that seem to warn the visitor to stay away. Their facial expressions, reinforced by their carriage, suggest surly, impassive, bad temper. They guard the sanctuary with tight-lipped, hostile menace. Their demeanour suggests that what they guard is a lower and *daimonic* order, a chaotic chthonic order. Their religious sanctuary is dark and half-underground: one where the power dwells. *Erechthonius* also means, literally, 'the very chthonic one', 'the deeply subterranean one'.[5] The Karyatids look straight up at the Parthenon, unimpressed, warning us not to be carried away by it.

And, as every student of Western civilisation knows, there is plenty to be carried away by. The contours of its perfection gave birth to an ethos. Here stands the archetype of classicism. Mathematical achievement is represented in its geometrical virtuosity, highlighted in the visual tricks whereby what seem the straight verticals of the columns and the horizontal plane of the podium base are, in fact, optical illusions. The platform on which the columns are seated is convex; the entablature, which spans the top of them, supporting the roof, is curved. The column shafts are not straight, but swell out in the middle; and the perimeter ones do not stand exactly vertical, but tilt inwards. The corner columns are thicker than the others. Every block of stone had to be cut on site to exact specifications.

Modern scholars agree that a temple as large as the Parthenon would look dull and lifeless if it were based on straight lines, precise right angles, and evenly spaced columns.[6] In what Iktinos designed there is a lightness and gravity, a magical vitality, giving the building a living, sculptural feel. It has been called a sculptor's temple. The architect outlined his principles in a lost book that the Roman architect Vitruvius had available to him. (We can get some sense of those principles from Vitruvius's own theory.)

What faces the visitor is *proportion*, visually projected in three dimensions. There is the ratio of length to width; there is the further ratio of height to the rectangular horizontal plane that it projects vertically, but not too far; and there are the proportions of base to column, column to capital, and capitals to frieze and pediment. The ratio of 9:4 governs many of these relationships: base length to width; base width to height of column, from foot to top of the cornice; and the axial spacing of columns to column diameter.[7] The Greeks had a theory of the 'commensurability of parts' that seems to have governed the design of the Parthenon.

Of the four cardinal virtues postulated by Plato and Aristotle, there is much in ancient Greek culture that would single out *sōphrosunē* as the first among equals. From Homer's writings to the Delphic 'nothing in excess', the first law was moderation, temperance — above all, balance. The Parthenon is *sōphrosunē* as architecture. If there is a supreme beauty in the perfection of mathematical laws, as Bertrand Russell reflected,[8] this is nowhere better exemplified than in Euclidean geometry. The finite proportions of Euclidean geometry, the sublime elegance of its proofs, were prefigured in the Parthenon.

The Parthenon makes explicit its homage to *sōphrosunē* in the sculptures that adorn it. They suggest to us the nature of Periklean religion, in stories overseen by Perikles' friend, Pheidias. Previous Greek temples were adorned with static images of the gods, or formulaic retellings of myths. Around the outside of the Parthenon run a band of *metopes* — that is, indented square spaces each containing a sculpture. These bands present four story-cycles, one by one, as they run along the sides of the temple. All proclaim the necessary victory of balance and measure over excess and barbarism.

There is the battle between the gods and giants, with the gods defeating primitive violence; there is the battle of proto-human Lapiths with brutish Centaurs; there is the war of Greeks against Trojans; and there is the defeat of Amazons at the hands of Athenians. In the commanding sculptures in the triangular pediments at each end of the Parthenon are depicted the birth of Athena out of her father's head, and her defeat of Poseidon. Finally, friezes around the internal rooms depict Athenians themselves in their everyday lives.[9] The modern viewer can see from the works that survive, especially those housed in the British Museum in London, craftsmanship of a quality that breathes a living vitality and intimate realism into the stone figures — a quality that reflects the humanist confidence of classical Athens.

Perikles had strong secular proclivities. And the philosopher Protagoras — famous for the humanist maxim, 'man is the measure of all things' — was a close friend. So it needs explaining why such a great rationalist as Perikles should have spent much of the wealth accumulated by the new Athenian empire on a religious building, containing a statue to a goddess. It was as if he was turning his own ideal Athens into the first example of 'civil religion'.[10] And, indeed, the Parthenon did not function as a temple — it had no altar. It never drew the Athenians to it in reverence as a sanctuary in which to pay homage to Athena.

Perikles did assert in his funeral oration that, 'We have no need of a Homer to praise us.' He himself, through his monuments, seems to have taken over the role of the rhapsodic poet. And the Parthenon sculptures do promote humans, making them fit to move among the gods, almost as their equals. The frieze shows Athenians at work, at war, at sport, playing music, parading on horseback, in religious procession, carrying the *peplos* to adorn Athena Polias, and conversing with their heroes. It idealises them, and at all ages, from spritely boys and girls, to handsome young men and pure maidens, to distinguished elders. It provides an immortal text in stone celebrating the virtues of the Athenians.[11]

Sōphrosunē, broken down etymologically, means 'saving mind'. It has no moral dimension. Classical Greek culture was not, in its primary mode, ethical. Protagoras, the teacher of Socrates, taught that Zeus had distributed two virtues to all humans: reverence and right.[12] So Perikles' friend had already separated the religious from the ethical — the good life for humans lies in revering the gods and obeying what is right.

In the next stage of what we might call metaphysical history, 'reverence' is reconfigured as 'balance'. This is the Delphic moment in Greek culture, linked with Apollo. Perhaps the suggestion is that 'reverence' is not what is normally regarded as religious, then as now — it is neither devotion (kneeling in prayer) nor ritual (sacrificing in temples). It is, rather, a state within the individual of higher composure, of receptiveness to the divine. For that, there has to be inner poise — what is actually meant by 'saving mind'. So *balance* is a religious state of being.

The prototypical individual in Greek tragedy is Oedipus; indeed, Aristotle framed his theory of tragedy around his story. Oedipus (to whom I shall return in the next chapter) killed his father and married his mother. But these moral transgressions are not his principal crimes. Rather, he is cursed for having violated a higher, metaphysical order: he sought to outsmart his fate, in an excess of self-confidence. After consulting the Oracle, he journeyed down from Delphi, and came across his unrecognised father at a

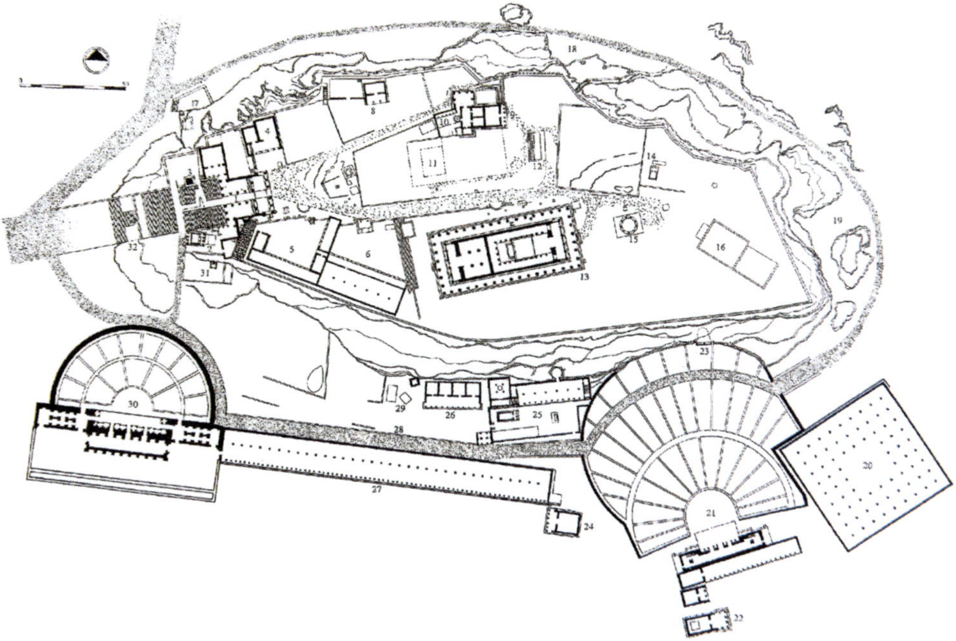

1. Propylaia
2. Sanctuary of Athena Nike
3. Monument of Eumenes II (later, of Agrippa)
4. Northwest Building
5. Sanctuary of Artemis Brauronia
6. Chalkotheke
7. Bronze Athena
8. Building III (House of the Arrhephoroi)
9. Erechtheion
10. Pandroseion
11. Opisthodomos?
12. Altar of Athena
13. Parthenon
14. Sanctuary of Zeus Polieus
15. Temple of Roma and Augustus
16. Building IV (Heroon of Pandion?)
17. Klepsydra Fountain
18. Shrine of Aphrodite and Eros
19. Cave of Aglauros
20. Odeion of Pericles
21. Theatre of Dionysos
22. Temple of Dionysos
23. Monument of Thrasyllos
24. Monument of Nikias
25. Asklepieion
26. Ionic Stoa
27. Stoa of Eumenes II
28. Boundary of the Spring
29. Temples of Isis and Themis
30. Odeion of Herodes Atticus
31. Sanctuary of Aphrodite Pandemos
32. Beulé Gate

From Hurwit, pp. 2–3

PLAN OF THE ACROPOLIS

spot where the three ways met. Here, on the lower slopes of Apollo's mountain, he killed his father, thereby violating both Delphic injunctions, 'Know thyself!' and 'Nothing in excess!' Oedipus is the human individual out of balance.

The Parthenon takes 'measure' to a higher order. 'Measure' becomes a virtue. The temple gives form to a *virtue* that supersedes morals or, to use Nietzsche's pregnant phrase, goes 'beyond good and evil'. To call this virtue 'aesthetic' demeans it. It is rather *virtue transcendent*. The clarity of the blue Athenian light on high above the city bathes the warm, cream-white stone, gleaming like the eyes of Athena. Shining, it presides, just like Achilles shines, as described in Book 18 of the *Iliad*, after Athena has bathed his head in golden, flaming light; and just like Jesus is described as Shining by Mark, when transfigured up on the mountain.

The Parthenon contrasts with the city below and around: a dingy, grubby, sprawling mess — now as then. Classical Athens was notorious for its private squalor. Perikles himself would die from a plague that swept the city in 429 BC. The public grandeur of the Parthenon is up and above, a semi-divine inspiration and a mockery of mortal inferiority. This is starkly to be observed in Athens today, with modern Greeks intimidated by what looms above them. The bar has been set so high that any but the most exceptionally gifted and confident are condemned to lower their heads and mutter, 'What can we possibly do to match this?' Pride in the past becomes paralysing, and streaked with resentment.

And, yet again, it was the ancient Greeks who help us to understand the problem. In Racine's seventeenth-century play *Phèdre* (which is itself a reworking of Euripides' Greek tragedy *Hippolytus*), the central character, Hippolytus, who is the son of Theseus, laments over his fate, and in particular over what he can possibly do in the shadow of his father, who has achieved everything — Theseus the hero of mythic grandeur, conqueror of the Amazons, killer of the Minotaur, saviour and founder of his city, Athens.[13] It was a curse to be born Hippolytus. It may be a curse to be born in the shadows of the Parthenon, and not just for contemporary Athenians. Modern Western high culture is riddled with resentment against its own preceding masterpieces, challenging the value of 'classical works'. Modern nihilism — costumed as relativism, critical theory, post-modernism, and deconstruction — is a manifestation of rancour against the authoritative past, rancour against the Parthenon.

The Parthenon is not Faustian, in the sense of a restless reaching ever upwards to the infinite — exemplified, as Oswald Spengler noted, in the Gothic cathedral.[14] The classical form is measured: the ratio of 9:4 limits the height. The comparison is instructive, and may help us to understand why the Parthenon is so intimidating. The great Gothic cathedrals also make any individual who enters them feel small and insignificant, but the contrast they set up is between man and God. They, too, are creations of such extraordinary grandeur it seems impossible, even to the modern eye, that mere mortals can have built them. They evoke a parallel ambivalence — both architectural master-works inspire mortals, while at the same time spotlighting their puniness.

Yet the main function of the Gothic cathedral is to lift the human spirit up, not to challenge it: the spirit soaring above the self, in awed reverence, to meet the divine. The cathedral is oriented unequivocally towards the heavens, whereas the Parthenon reflects a more this-worldly relationship to human society. It is both above the city and a part of it.

The Parthenon sets up its own polarity. It ranks humans and

their societies. It distinguishes those who are rare and exceptional from those who are normal and ordinary. Or, perhaps more accurately put, it projects an ethos with this discriminating bite. It challenges: *Your ancestors conceived me, and built me, using their supreme human powers of reason, imagination, and will. Dare to measure up to them! Dare to build something so beautifully perfect! Dare to charm the presiding goddess!*

The Parthenon has its own counter-balance, equivalent to the chasm projected in the Gothic cathedral between almighty God and petty, miserable, and sinful mortals. It is in the earthy caution nearby. The Karyatids glower up at the Parthenon. They charge humans not to get too carried away with the classical sublime, and with fantasies of death-defying achievement.

The Parthenon is without precedent. There is no equivalent motif in the *Iliad*, although there is perhaps some hint of the rational order to come in the *Odyssey*, with the brilliant stratagems of Odysseus that climax in him, virtually single-handedly, and after careful planning, defeating the horde of suitors and killing them all. And the way is partly prepared by the resolution to the spiralling cycle of retribution in Aeschylus's *Oresteian Trilogy* (458 BC) — a cycle in which a king serves his brother pieces of his own children cooked in a pie, the next king kills his own daughter to satisfy an oracle, his wife kills him, and then their son kills her. The resolution occurs in Athens, in a court presided over by Athena, and involves an appeal to moderation and balance. But Aeschylus's finale carries little of the shining, charismatic authority of the Parthenon.

In this, the Erechtheion is different. It has a long precedent, with its roots in archaic mythology, finally reaching its pinnacle in the Mycenaean horror, as recorded by Aeschylus the Athenian. Its chthonic is forever — the timeless subterranean, the dank imagined crypt inside which malevolent powers dwell.

The Acropolis, with its sacred buildings separated from the nether human chaos, is aloof, part way to being Olympian. When seen from afar, or from close below from the right angle, it is dominated by the Parthenon (see p. 180). The Erechtheion is more modest and inward — more an acquired taste. The Parthenon, crowning the Acropolis, is constitutive of *virtue transcendent*. It has inspired the highest Western achievements.

The personification of the goddess Athena sharpens the polarities. With the Parthenon, there emerges a new conception of the presiding goddess — or, should we call her, in our more plebeian modern idiom, the commanding spirit of the place and time, its higher ideal.

Pheidias took nine years to make his statue, which came to be known as Athena Parthenos: Athena the maiden, or virgin.[15] It cost as much as the Parthenon itself — her flesh was made of ivory; her eyes, of precious stones and ivory; and her robe and equipment, of solid gold. She steadied a monumental shield leaning on the ground at her side: five metres in diameter, it was decorated on the inside with images of a battle of gods and giants, and on the outside with a battle of Greeks and Amazons revolving around a Gorgon's head. A giant snake, the mythic guardian of the Acropolis, was coiled beside her. A vertical spear rested against her left shoulder, while she held a gold-and-ivory image of Victory, itself two metres high, in her right hand — to celebrate the defeat of the Persians in 490 BC and 480 BC. The Parthenon was considerably enlarged over its predecessor so it could exhibit this colossal statue. The temple was designed to house the goddess, and likely came to take its name from the statue.

Actually, it was the temple itself, rather than the statue inside, that was the aesthetic masterpiece — the incarnation of *virtue transcendent*. The statue is long gone, without any trace of it left behind. But from later copies, including a modern one built to scale, housed in a replica Parthenon in Centennial Park in Nashville, it gives the strong impression of heavy volume and stolid, over-elaborate decoration. Athena Parthenos lacks poise or grace. A chunky monolith draped in gaudy stones and massive plates of gold, it may be our gain that she is lost while her temple remains.

Athena's shield was otherwise known as the fearful *aegis*, made from goat hide, that was given to her by her father, Zeus. The shield had the face of the Medusa sewn into its centre, the eyes looking forward. Perseus slew the Medusa, one of the Gorgon sisters, chopping off its head — the female monster with writhing snakes for hair, the monster whose gaze would turn any human who caught its eye to stone. So Athena, goddess of wisdom, truth goddess, has the symbolic power to kill when approached in the wrong way. She kills by petrifaction. In her virginity, chaste by choice, she is the cool (and cunningly smart) one among the deities — cool but not frigid like Artemis, Apollo's sister, who was associated with moon and night.

Plato, in his *Cratylus* Dialogue, notes the etymology of her name as 'the mind of god' — *ē-theo-noa* — or, 'she who knows divine things better than others'.[16] On the one hand, she was the divinity identified with crafty and practical intelligence — which she shares with one of her human protégés, Odysseus. On the other hand, her wisdom is sacred knowledge; it is not in the rational,

RECONSTRUCTION MODEL OF ATHENA PARTHENOS

Socratic mode. So it was that the olive became sacred. It became the fuel for the golden light. Indeed, Strabo and Pausanias, after visits to Athens, both reported that Athena Polias, in the Erechtheion, was illuminated by an ever-burning oil lamp — Plutarch calls it the 'sacred lamp', the Lamp of Athena.

Thus Athena looks two ways, also gesturing towards the Erechtheion, her other sanctuary, where the eternal lamp burns — one steeped in powerful homage to her. Like it, she can be dark. Why otherwise give her the Gorgon? This monstrous woman's face stares out through her hair of writhing snakes: she is a demonic, animate gargoyle, her mouth open, her teeth gleaming, the menace she radiates alternating between one of devouring attack and petrifaction. The Medusa belongs in the Erechtheion as its guarding mystery, like the Minotaur dwelling in the depths of the Knossos Palace in Crete. If you wish to approach 'the mind of god' and its sacred wisdom — as any mortal would — the Medusa warns you to tread with ultimate care, approaching from the right angle, for the wrong glimpse will turn you to stone. It is all about how to look.

Athena invented the horse bridle and the ox-yoke. These gifts tame brute strength — tossing, prancing, galloping energy — and allow humanity to harness horsepower to its own ends. She bridles, symbolically, the more primitive god Poseidon. Poseidon, on one occasion metamorphosed into a stallion, had mated with the Medusa, who had a mare's body. Athena provided Perseus with a mirror, which allowed him to look at the Medusa without being turned to stone; thereby he was able to kill her. The wise goddess wanted the power of the Gorgon look for herself. At every turn of this complex mythology, she outsmarts Poseidon for her own ends.

The metaphor of the bridle extends into allusions to self-control, as in Athena's own self-imposed chastity. But the bridle

MEDUSA, C 510 BC

and the yoke are also symbols of *anagkē* — Necessity. *Necessity* was identified by the ancient Greeks as female, and more powerful than any of the gods. Her most direct impact on human life was through her daughters, the three Fates. Fate binds, and the thread of each individual destiny may not be stretched or cut. Humans are mere oxen yoked to their given fates.[17] Athena endorses this truth.

Athena is uncompromising. Her gleaming eyes control every encounter. She is a warrior goddess, characteristically wearing a helmet, holding a shield, and carrying a spear, perhaps to signal that everything she presides and watches over is a battle. If we look one way, we see a wrestle to gain *virtue transcendent*. Her Parthenon sets the ideal — there is something chaste and pure about it. If we look the other way, we see a wrestle to gain the Karyatid truths — dark, brooding, and fated.

The human individual is left to integrate the two domains, to bring them into some sort of harmony within which it is possible to live. It is as if the higher self dwells on top of the Acropolis, seeking to worship in one temple and then the other, without contradiction. The Greeks imagined their gods living on top of Mt Olympus. In my picture here, it is as if the higher human self in the West, including its own fragment of divinity, dwells on top of another mountain (a comparatively diminutive one, as is appropriate) — the Acropolis in Athens.

The ancient Athenians had their own ways of mediating between the two worlds. A massive open-air altar — dedicated to Athena Polias — stood between the Parthenon and the Erechtheion, at the east end (see p. 31). It was where the Panathenaic procession, on the opening night of the great annual festival in Athens, would end, reaching its climax with the arrival of a torch race bringing fire. A hundred cows (a hekatomb) were then sacrificed on the altar.

This was a wild, evocative climax, with bellowing cows, the ritual screaming of women, thick smoke, the seductive aroma of roasting meat, burning fat, rivers of blood pouring across the rock — all of this accompanying drinking, feasting, singing, and dancing, continuing on through the warm summer night.[18] Close by, on guard, was the towering silhouette of the Parthenon, and equally the earthier, chthonic shadow of the Erechtheion, fire and torch-light sending the reflections of unleashed human passion across marble columns, mingling with the sculptures, as if conjoined in a dance of gods, heroes, and mortals. The band of sculptures up above the revellers, along the north side of the Parthenon, depicted scenes from the Trojan War.

This annual night of revelry on the Acropolis was held in close proximity to the classical paradigm of Restraint — just as the Trojan War was conducted under the god-sanctioned law of 'nothing in excess'. Athena was the patron of just war, in contrast with Ares, the war-god who championed the berserk brutishness of tribal, man-slaughtering excess. The law that presides here is that there shall be balance. The olive symbolises the flowing oil of prosperity and the olive branch of peace. Athena's own balancing is represented in her special liking for both the supreme warrior, Achilles, and the man of intelligent and eloquent craftiness, Odysseus. At key moments, she would bathe each of them in her golden light.

The Athenians were writing their own story. It would set the mythic parameters — in stone, in ritual, and in deed — for how they would understand themselves. Hence, as Perikles asserted, they had no need of a Homer to provide the narrative for them. The Acropolis structured the story. It established a driving polarity, the source of the creative friction that gives birth to culture: any culture, not just theirs.[19]

Here, we have entered the domain of *mythos* — the body of timeless stories from a long time ago that gives shape to a culture. These stories bear the stamp of eternity for a people, setting the terms in which they would ideally like to live. In fact, for the Athenians, whatever Perikles said, the *mythos* was heavily indebted to Homer. For one, the all-night revelries on top of the Acropolis on the first night of the Panathenaic Festival were conducted under a line of sculptures depicting scenes from the Trojan War. These were scenes from Homer: fighting heroes on high; drunken mortals, below.

The Parthenon as *virtue transcendent* conjures up a dream, but that dream springs out of its concreteness. It is a dream that arises, shining, out of a timeless substantiality — one that has played the principal role in building a civilisation. It inspired a confident individualism that 'man is the measure of all things', ushering in a spirit of free enquiry, and it led to the scientific method, civic democracy, and a striving to create and master beautiful forms.

For example, let me take one component: the Pnyx. This open-air site in Athens, where democracy was born, took the form of a grassy plateau on the side of a hill 500 metres from the Acropolis, opposite the front of it. It had the capacity to hold 6000 citizens — the place appears very much today as it would have in the fifth-century BC, free public space where anyone can walk, or sit for a while and contemplate. The Athenians would gather here to debate the affairs of state, having positioned themselves so that the Parthenon on high watched over their politics, blessing and legitimising their civic gatherings. Protagoras exemplifies Athenian practical wisdom, by including in his story of Zeus giving *reverence* and *right* to humans the stipulation that they be given to all men, because cities would not survive if only an elite few shared in these virtues.

At times, the Athenians displayed their own practical wisdom here. There was the extraordinary occasion in 483 BC when Themistokles addressed the assembly. The Athenians had just discovered that their silver mines were vastly richer than they had thought. The ruling Council had announced it would put a proposal to keep half of the silver in the treasury and divide the other half equally among the 30,000 citizens — 10 drachmas per head. For the 20,000 citizens without land, 10 drachmas was a major windfall. On the morning in question, the forty-year-old Themistokles was the first to mount the speaker's platform. He argued that the silver would be better spent building a navy—100 new triremes (warships propelled by three tiers of oars). He persuaded the majority of citizens to vote against their own short-term interest.

The navy was built just in time to defeat the Persian invasion three years later. This day in 483 BC is arguably without equal in the long history of democracy. If the Persians had won in 480 BC, there most probably would have been no Athenian Golden Age, and few of the masterpieces that it made possible, including the Parthenon.[20]

The Parthenon also presides over the foundation of Western philosophy. Socrates taught in the streets below. Plato, a student of Socrates, and his own student Aristotle, institutionalised their work in teaching universities in Athens — in the Academy and the Lyceum. To put this in perspective, there is some cogency to Alfred North Whitehead's famous remark that the entirety of Western philosophy is merely a series of footnotes to Plato.[21]

Whilst Greek culture was not primarily ethical, moral philosophy plays an important role in Plato's work, as it does in that of Aristotle. In particular, Plato and Aristotle together establish the notion of four character virtues, two of which centre on the ethical: a sense of justice, and a capacity for practical thinking. The other two virtues are obliquely ethical: courage, and moderation or balance.

But it is Socrates who was the principal moral philosopher. The Socrates portrayed by Plato in the Dialogues focused on the days just preceding his death, argues that the purpose of human life is to act justly, avoiding doing harm to others. The method for so living is *rational*, with individuals admonished to spend their days examining themselves and what they contemplate doing, so as to determine whether it is right in the given circumstances. Free individuals should then act on their understanding.

In the person of Socrates, a major new player steps onto the stage of Western culture. About 2300 years later, Nietzsche provides the interpretative cue for this development, identifying Socrates with three maxims: knowledge is virtue; man sins only from ignorance; and he who is virtuous is happy. Reason is the pre-eminent human power. Through it, humans can think their way to goodness, and they can change who they are. That is, they can reform being.[22] This is a huge claim. It will reverberate down through the history of the West, giving intellectual legitimacy to the optimistic view that we, as individuals, can change ourselves for the better. It is diametrically at odds with the message of Oedipus and Delphi.

Socrates' picture of the moral life is different from that found normally within religious cultures. It is not predicated on religious rewards and punishments — on the logic that if I behave well, I will receive gifts from the spirits, the gods, or from God. It contrasts notably with the Catholic view that the virtuous will be rewarded at death by going to heaven, and the wicked punished by descending into hell. Roman Catholic doctrine pivots on providing religious rewards for leading a moral life.

For Socrates, humans should follow what is good, and avoid what is evil, for virtue's own sake. Acting justly is an end in itself. It is constitutive of being human. Moreover, Socrates argues that the main purpose of wisdom is to help individuals behave morally.

Socrates further assumes that the good will be happy. Given that sticking to moral principles can lead, at the extreme, to martyrdom — as was to happen to Socrates himself — his notion of 'happiness' clearly does not equate with pleasure, or with the avoidance of pain. He rather implies that there is some kind of inner fulfilment in being a just person. In other words, acting ethically carries within itself its own transcendence, its own higher justification. It stands as a manifestation of *virtue transcendent*.

Socrates founded a secular morality that would reverberate through Western history. It is, finally, in modern times that his view of the moral law as universal and absolute, and quite independent from religious belief, has come into preponderance.

In fact, Socrates was not the sole originator of rational moral philosophy. A similar perspective is found in other classical Greek philosophies, and especially in Stoicism. And its position within the cultural form incarnate in the Parthenon needs to be qualified. The later Plato would himself move into a more religious conception of the human condition. In his last work, *The Laws*, he stresses, as central to education, the cultivation of 'right fear' — reverence for what should be revered, and abhorrence of what should be abhorred.[23] Here, Plato comes to a much broader sense of 'law' than its ethical dimension, with some kind of sacred order predominating over the moral one.

This late Plato has a closer affinity with the Parthenon than his Socrates does: its shining presence casts 'measure' and 'balance' as non-ethical virtues. What it projects is more like *eurutbmia*, as celebrated by the Greeks — 'beautiful rhythm'.[24] The Parthenon itself stands at once as a masterpiece of human creation and as a temple in honour of the supreme goddess. Here, in Athens, is the classical paradigm for finding concrete symbolic form for the 'mind of god'.

The Karyatids act as the necessary counter-force to *virtue transcendent*. Who, then, are these six maidens? They may get their name from Karyai, a state in the Peloponnese that had sided, in the early fifth century, with the invading Persians. The Greeks later took revenge by storming Karyai, killing the men, and taking the women into slavery. Vitruvius reports that architects then included statues of these enslaved women in public buildings, carrying a load symbolising the weight of their shame, recording for posterity the transgression of Karyai.[25] In Athens, they do stand above the site of the old temple dedicated to victory in 490 BC at Marathon over the Persians under Darius, the temple that had been destroyed in 480 BC by the Persians in their second invasion, when they were led by Xerxes. Perhaps the statues do survey the vanished ruins, symbolic of the women's shame.

However, similar Karyatid maidens are also to be found on earlier Greek temples, ones predating the Persian wars. The prosaic interpretation is that they represent everyday life, of women carrying water-jars on their heads.

I am more interested in the evocative power of the Karyatid

maidens — their dramatic effect. I see three ghostly presences behind their collective look. There is, firstly, the Medusa, the Gorgon sister killed by Perseus. She represents the Athena eye unveiled. When the goddess raises her shield, it is not in self-defence: it is to target some unfortunate mortal.

What might the power to turn a person to stone signify? The Perseus story is loaded with castration imagery.[26] Petrifaction evokes emasculation, the loss of all vitality and power. The hero is prophesied to kill his grandfather (symbolically his father, in that his actual father is Zeus, king of the gods). Perseus enacts his fate, in a family parallel with Zeus having overthrown his own father, Chronos, who had himself gained power after castrating his father, Uranus.

Perseus represents the potentially emasculated son, who has grown up in close confinement with his mother, literally — as a baby he was thrown into the sea nailed up inside a casket with her. He has to prove himself by overcoming a series of powerful females, thus asserting his manhood. Chopping off the head of the Medusa alludes to castration, in that it kills her potency. The Medusa is typically portrayed in Greek art with a wide-open devouring mouth — a gaping black hole surrounded by prominent teeth.[27] She represents, in part, the dominating, biting, castrating mother. Perhaps one reason for Athena's chastity was, from the human, and especially male, perspective, to remove the sexual threat.

The Athenians demonstrated their own fearful obsession with powerful women in their fascination with the legendary tribe of warrior women, the Amazons. The Amazons dominated their husbands, who kept house. The founder of Athens, Theseus, defeated the Amazons and got them to revert to their 'normal' female roles.[28] For Athenians, to represent their victory over the Amazons in the Parthenon sculptures seems like a way of asserting their precarious masculinity. Likewise, there is a psychosexual logic to their attachment to Athena — a chaste woman who supports everything male but marriage.[29] She was the perfect divine projection for the heavily misogynist culture of Athens. That Athena, the 'mother' of Athens, was herself not born of woman only confirmed the deep local ambivalence towards the feminine.

However, a one-dimensional Freudian reading is inadequate here. For it is equally true that the Athenians displayed a profound engagement with, and understanding of, the feminine. They chose Athena as their presiding divinity. They chose, as their founding symbol, the olive, with its subtle feminine associations, over the masculinity of the horse. And the principal figures celebrated on the Acropolis are all female, from Athena, represented in many prominent sculptures, to numerous statues of Nike (Victory), to the Karyatids.

The west pediment of the Parthenon illustrates all this in sculpture. It depicts the battle between Poseidon and Athena for the soul of Athens. Poseidon is a primitive, masculine, pre-Olympian divinity, with his attributes representative of the barbaric past — he is god of the most violent extremes of nature in earthquakes and raging, ship-wrecking storms at sea. Further, the metopes around the Parthenon narrate the struggle between civilisation and barbarism, just as the temple as a whole is dedicated to the Greek victory over what were seen as the semi-human barbarians from the East, the Persians. Athena herself embodies the birth of human society out of the primeval woods. And, true to form, the birth of Athena is depicted on the east, or front, pediment of the Parthenon. According to Hesiod, the forming of the world — creation — ends with her birth.

To return to the specifics of the Gorgon, there is a dialectical play on *stone*. One way, the living human becomes petrified; the other way, the stone image is brought to life by the sculptor's inspiration. The Karyatids are themselves stone images — stone impregnated with sacred persona. As the profane material is metamorphosed one way, turning into a living power, so too, inversely, the spark of human divinity may be snuffed out. In dread at what the stony-faced Karyatids portend, human blood may freeze, paralysing the viewer with horror. But what manner of truth can it be that, once seen, the viewer would choose to turn to stone, rather than receive its message?[30]

The passion in humans that fuels abundant and enduring vitality depends on connection with the deep truths. One Greek metaphor was the transition from the brute war-god Ares and the satyr to Athena and the Karyatids — from the virility of bestial lust and sadism, which sate themselves in exhaustion, to the tragic grandeur that makes us fully human.

Athena, by proxy, kills off the primeval monster-female — the Medusa — but then takes over her power. The goddess proceeds to use this force with controlled effect. The Gorgon look had been, in its primitive form, berserkly anarchic and undiscriminating, as symbolised by its hair-halo of writhing snakes. Athena does not civilise the Medusa; she rather projects the Gorgon menace into the full human experience.

The Greek view was that we humans instinctively prefer to live in a state of oblivion — or permanent forgetfulness — with eyes lowered and blinkered, and with a deliberately short focus on the day-to-day. However, if I may use a biological simile, to live in oblivion is to live like those who isolate themselves inside sterilised rooms, and who, lacking routine exposure to germs, fail to build up antibodies, thus rendering themselves vulnerable to fatal disease the moment they step out into life. So it is that evasion of Karyatid truths means that the six maidens, when they do manifest themselves like avenging spectres, may paralyse the defenceless victim. The goddess of truth is lethal. She obliterates not with her spear, but with her haunting-eyed shield, which she raises to target those who seek to evade her.

Journeying in Greece today, what exists of antiquity is limited almost entirely to creations in stone. So a larger question arises here, to accompany us as we proceed.

Looking at the Karyatids, the second presence I detect is that of the Furies of human destiny. Athena talked the Furies into taking up residence 'beside Erechtheus in his house' on the Acropolis, in a 'deep and subterranean hold'.[31] The Furies are primeval demonic spirits, which rise out of dark, prehistoric times to enact retribution. They are the avenging fates which ensure that each individual's script is fulfilled, having been born from the blood spilled onto the ground from the severed neck of the Medusa. Aeschylus put it thus in his *Oresteia*: 'The black Furies stalking the man fortunate beyond all right wrench back again the set of his life and drop him to darkness.'[32]

Sophocles, thirty years later than the *Oresteia*, in *Oedipus the King* (426 BC), separated the fates into two different clusters. There were the *moirai*, who wrote the script, and the *kēres*, who ensured that it was fulfilled. In English, we might distinguish them as the fates and the dooms.

The Furies transmit signals from a dark past brooding over the present, one from which it is impossible to escape. What horrors lie embedded within, beneath the veneer of order and beauty! When Athena triumphs over Poseidon, her Shining helmet sparks *virtue transcendent*. But the Parthenon is not left alone on the Acropolis. In the European eighteenth century, it would become the naive

Enlightenment fantasy that the Parthenon, and its Empire of Reason, might rule solely and supremely over the human condition. This Enlightenment fantasy sought to deny the dark maidens; and in France, its place of origin, it would usher in, not its own ideals of universal brotherhood and peace, but the Revolution, the Terror, and Napoleon. It was as if the Furies had returned, in vengeance. In this, the Athenians were wiser than the men of the Enlightenment.

Well, some Athenians were. Socrates was the forefather of the Enlightenment. The eighteenth-century Parisians who worshipped at the temple of the new Virtue chose him as their presiding authority, their charismatic patron-saint. Jacques-Louis David painted Socrates in 1787 as the Messiah of Reason, martyred for his cause. The Karyatid view of all this is easy to imagine. No one could be an object of greater scorn in their eyes than Socrates. The six of them, in all their brooding mass, single out for special contempt those humans who believe, in their disaffection with themselves, and with their condition, that they can change. The dream of reforming being — the dream that tomorrow morning my caterpillar self will wake up metamorphosed into a butterfly — is the greatest of all saving lies. It feeds into the modern ideal of freedom: that I am free to make myself as I will. Repressing the tragic, it is in denial of the deep enigma of what it is to be human. It betrays the responsibility that comes with being born human. It was Socrates who gave authority to this lie, a lie that would develop into a major strand in Western belief.[33]

The Karyatids are thirdly, and finally, Kassandra. The chaste, beautiful daughter of King Priam of Troy, she was cursed by Apollo to see the future, but lived in a state of bitter loneliness because no one would believe her prophecies. At the gates of Mycenae, brought there as Agamemnon's slave concubine after the fall of Troy, she foresees that the queen, Klytemnestra, is about to slaughter her, and, with her, King Agamemnon. She likens her fate to 'the sheer edge of the tearing iron'.[34] As she herself puts it, her song of high-pitched wailing lament, and truth, stands in antithesis to the sweet tune of the nightingale. If only to be like the bird, carefree and joyful!

Kassandra is able to brace herself and, now composed, to announce, 'I will take my fate.' She descends from Agamemnon's chariot, and begins her slow, solitary walk through the Lion Gate into the fortress of Mycenae. Kassandra gains a higher strength from her knowledge. The deep truths connect her to an order beyond her mortal self which, like her song, rises above the incomprehensible, dark chaos of the human plane.[35]

What Kassandra sees would turn any normal person to stone. It strikes me that it is *her* wisdom that possesses the grim, glowering faces of the Karyatids. Their forbidding look seems to warn of dangerous knowledge. Kassandra implies that no human should want her prophetic gift. Yet everyone is cursed with an unconscious knowing that sends tremors back from the future to unsettle the present.

The Karyatids are impregnated with culture. It is the culture of what Kassandra describes with the Greek word *ainigma*, which translates as something like 'dark saying'. Kassandra speaks culture as necessity. The Medusa lurks just behind her; the Furies swarm overhead; and the olive is at her right hand. As culture, this is deeply mysterious, obscure, cryptic, and profound — just what the Parthenon is not.

The Parthenon as Shining is checked by the Karyatids. They act as the counter-force, the negative pole that generates the cultural current. The resulting fusion — of the Parthenon with the Karyatids — is the dynamic source of the culture of the West.

MYCENAE, LION GATE

V. Svolopoulos, from Petsas 2004, p. 32.

RECONSTRUCTION OF THE SANCTUARY OF APOLLO, DELPHI

THREE

DELPHI

The most likely way to travel to Delphi today is by car or bus from Athens via Thebes, but it is the wrong way in *mythos* terms. The traveller will be tempted to stop en route in Thebes, given its former glory as one of the major cities in ancient Greece and the fact that it was the setting of the Theban cycle of stories, which provided nearly half of the content for classical tragedy — the Trojan War being the other major contributor. However, modern Thebes is a squalid, charmless town, and, in my opinion, is not worth a pause. Having passed through it, and advanced well along the road into the region of Phokis, it is just as one starts to climb the lower slopes of Mt Parnassus — the sacred mountain — that one comes to the point where the famous three roads met. Sophocles makes it clear that this was not a crossroads. It was, rather, a narrow spot at which the road forked.

Oedipus, when he visited Delphi to consult the Oracle, would have come from the opposite direction. His journey began in Corinth, where he had grown up as the son of the king and queen. He would have arrived, presumably by boat, at Kirrha, the ancient port of Delphi on the Gulf of Corinth (today it is a small town called Itea). From Kirrha, he had to climb up a steep track to Delphi, which hovered on the side of the mountain six hundred metres above the Gulf. Once there, he gained admittance to Apollo's Temple, where the Oracle delivered her dreadful prophecy: he would kill his father, marry his mother, and sire with her children cursed by their incestuous origins.

Oedipus fled Delphi in the opposite direction from which he had come — understandably, to get as far away from his parents as he could — in the direction of Thebes. Descending the track down the mountain on foot, he arrived at where the three ways meet. He had the choice of either of two directions: Daulia, off to the left, or Thebes, straight ahead.

The choice was made for him — by finding himself plunged into an angry encounter with a traveller, who, unprovoked, forced him off the road, then hit him over the head with a heavy stick as he passed by in his chariot. Oedipus, in a fit of rage, killed the man, whom he did not recognise as his father, Laius. The truth was that Oedipus had been put out at birth on a hillside to die, his ankles pierced and tied together (because his father had been told the same prophecy). The baby was found and saved by a shepherd servant of the King of Corinth.

Oedipus, after killing his unknown father, might still have chosen Daulia. But who has heard of this small, obscure village — then as now? It represented the choice of nowhere, of a quiet life, of oblivion. Today, driving on the road from Thebes, just short of where the ancient three ways met, one comes to a crossroads. The signpost off to the right reads 'Daulia'. With Delphi beckoning straight ahead, and above, who could take the right fork?

Let us linger a moment with Oedipus. He is everyman, the ideal man — according to reputation, the 'greatest of men'. He should prepare us well for what awaits us at the top of the road winding up the mountain. For his life was determined from Delphi, the centre of the world around which it orbited. He sought to free himself from its dreadful centripetal pull, its sucking vortex of implacability, but failed. Everyone who walks in his shoes fails with him.

Oedipus's failure was spectacular. On that very journey of freedom as he sped down the mountain to escape his fate, he became trapped at a narrow pass in the road, jammed in by his father's carriage, hit over the head by what had to be. Kassandra would have smiled knowingly. By the end of his journey, Oedipus too might proclaim, 'I will take my fate.' Here is part of his greatness.

Oedipus's failure is exemplary, and it stands, by the completion of the story, as the most demanding warning to mortals in the entirety of Western literature.

Teiresias, the blind seer in the story who tells Oedipus the truth about himself, has as his opening words, 'Woe, woe, to know is terrible.' The inner sight, the clarity that is wisdom, is terrible. Nietzsche would paraphrase this Greek tragic view as, 'Wisdom is a crime against nature.'[1]

Teiresias lost his sight, according to one story, because he stumbled on Athena bathing. She blinded him, but then partly relented, having one of the snakes from her aegis lick his ears, giving him the gift of prophecy. To see Athena naked turns a man to stone — to look on naked truth petrifies the beholder. Or perhaps Teiresias voluntarily blinded himself so as not to gaze into the eyes of the Medusa. Teiresias wants sacred knowledge, but not to pay the

DELPHI: TEMPLE OF APOLLO

price for it. Oedipus will deliberately stab out his own eyes, with his wife/mother's gold brooches, when he finds out the horror of who he is. His life has been a steady and remorseless journey, unveiling the Medusa. He withstands the look. Legend has it that a monster lived under the place where the three ways meet.

But let us proceed up the mountain to Delphi. The Greeks set their most religious site in nature, well away from centres of population and trade. Delphi was very difficult to get to; it challenged the transport of heavy building-materials. Yet pilgrims came from the distant reaches of the known world to consult the Oracle — and, once there, were willing to wait months for an answer to their questions. King Croesus journeyed from Lydia in Asia Minor. Delphi was more than pan-Hellenic; it was global and, as such, unique at the time. The Oracle's riddles were famously misunderstood, thereby increasing its reputation. Even Oedipus, who did not receive an ambiguous prophecy — what he was told was all too plain — got it fatefully wrong. He may have been better off to linger in Delphi, but then that, too, would have been to defy what was coming.

Perhaps the Oracle was itself a bit beside the point. Its deeper function may have been to serve as an inducement, or excuse, to come here and enter into the presence of the gods. The message, encrypted in the notorious ambiguity of the Oracle, was then not to dwell in the particular — but simply to come and breathe the Delphic air.

Delphi is closer to the gods than is the Acropolis. The ethos is more rarefied. The still tang of its mountain air braces the visitor. There is an eerie enchantment here, as if one has left the human plane and entered an adult version of a fairytale land, the witches and wolves replaced by a pervasive, resonant, and sacred force. That force charges the air, which hovers like an invisible canopy over the site. It has a different quality to that found anywhere else. The light is soft. A number of those who visit Delphi, myself included, find that it has the most powerful presence of any place they have ever been.

Yet Delphi is *sōphrosunē*. Set half-way up Mt Parnassus, it is in-between, neither peak nor plain, as if mediating between heaven and earth. That earth can be seen below, in the form of the Gulf of Corinth — and again it is far away, but not too far. The mountains of the Peloponnese, of Arcadia, rise in the distance.

Every pilgrim entering the ancient Oracle's domain, winding up the sacred way to Apollo's Temple, would have been met, once inside the temple antechamber, by the chiselled inscription, 'Nothing in excess'. *Sōphrosunē*, as command and warning, rules this place. It is set alongside Apollo's parallel injunction, 'Know thyself!'

But the site, centring on that temple, would, in its prime, have looked gaudy to our eyes — not measured. Much of the marble was painted. The sacred way leading up to the Oracle was cluttered with statues and Treasuries, themselves ornate minor temples decorated with painted friezes, sculptured metopes, and statues. Pausanias noted 3000 statues and 28 Treasuries in his time. Much of the sacred way would have seemed like ostentatious clutter, with tributes from different cities jockeying for prominence.

At the entrance to the complex was a huge bronze bull, with the way through being flanked on the right side by a line of nine bronze statues; on the left, 38 statues contributed to the Spartan Monument. Further on, up the way, an assortment of grand statues on high bases would have dwarfed the visitor — including a 16-metres-high Apollo, and, on a column standing 12 metres high, the refined and haughty marble Sphinx from Naxos, which can be admired today in the Delphi Museum.

There were multiple balances to check the ostentation. First, this is a site where human beings are put in their modest place by nature in its harsh Delphic mountain grandeur, with crags rising behind, the sweep of rocky hillsides below and, away to the right, the gorge beneath.

Second, Apollo's Temple itself, in its sixth-century-BC Doric simplicity, would have given the impression of hulking mass and masculine gravity — perhaps even unrefined heaviness — but not over-decorated show. It was the fifth temple built on the site, finished in 548–547 BC, and then rebuilt after an earthquake in 373 BC.[2]

As a third check, just above the temple is an amphitheatre, looking over it; and above the amphitheatre, privately set among trees, is an athletics stadium. We are reminded of the breadth and depth of ancient Greek religion. It featured festivals: in its Delphic mode, the Pythian Games. And those pan-Hellenic festivals celebrated great human feats, in which men transcended their normal selves. In the early years of the Pythian Games, which started in 586 or 582 BC, poetic hymns to Apollo were performed, accompanied by the lyre. Later, the Games developed into a seven-day festival. Days for sacrifice and for banqueting gave way to a day for contests in the high arts: musical hymns, tragedies, and comedies. Prizes for music and drama distinguished the Delphic Games from those at Olympia. The following day was devoted to sporting contests. As with the Acropolis, there was a celebration of the highest mental and physical human achievement. Here, human prowess, glory, and creative excellence were enabled within the precinct of vast, obscure, and determining religious forces.

Delphi is Apollo's domain. What do we know about the god himself, his attributes and associations? His name derives from *apelia*, making him the god of authoritative speech, or the word; the god of song and poetry. He is characteristically portrayed as an ephebe — youth-like, soft-skinned, beardless, and with shoulder-length hair. Apollo chases women, but usually fails.[3]

The lengthy *Homeric Hymn to Apollo* tells us much about him. He was born, with his twin sister, Artemis, on the sacred island of Delos. Apollo is linked with the sun; his chaste huntress sister, with the moon. At birth, he lays claim to the trio of music, archery, and prophecy. With the lyre, he brings harmony to Olympus; with the bow, he defends his father Zeus's interests without challenging him. His third domain, prophecy, allows him, as the *Hymn* puts it, to 'convey to mankind the unfailing will of Zeus'. His birth had brought fear on Olympus that the king god's son would inevitably grow up to challenge and overthrow the father, thus bringing instability, even chaos. Apollo breaks the cycle. He represents a new generation of divinities, instating civilised order.

Apollo, as lord of oracles, is all-knowing, and the god of truth. He hates lies and illusion. In association, he presides over purification rites. He is the leader of the Muses — the demi-goddesses who represent the arts. The number and nature of the Muses fluctuates depending on the ancient source, with Homer referring to only one. The most influential list came from Hesiod, who described nine — who inspired, in their turn, the epic form, history, flute-playing, lyric poetry, lyric poetry and dancing, tragedy, comedy, hymns and pantomime, and astronomy. Apollo, as conductor of the Muses, and as the god of the lyre, and music in general, commands the means through which the truth is voiced.[4]

From Delos, Apollo surveyed the earth, looking for a site for his Oracle. He decided on a rocky and infertile hillside where a savage serpent ruled, and, after some difficulty, managed to claim the site by shooting the dragon python with his bow. He had chosen the wild and inhospitable, a site with chthonic origins, linked with the primitive earth-goddess Gaia, with clefts, underground caverns, and vapours. Apollo had taken on the archaic, the female, and the monstrous, replacing them with balance and truth — with the voice of god speaking the future.[5] By stilling primeval violence and chaos, he played a parallel role in Greek culture to that of Athena, as she is represented in the Parthenon.

Apollo was linked with two cult places, Delos and Delphi, the two most sacred sites in the ancient Greek world. Neither had local cult associations. Apollo, like Jesus later, defended the universal human against the local, the tribal, and the xenophobic. The prestige of Delos and Delphi derived from their character as pan-Hellenic shrines, where men and women from across the known world came in peace to celebrate and consult the prophetic god.[6]

The first-century-AD essayist Plutarch served as a priest of Apollo at Delphi. He writes of the shrine, and in particular of the capital letter 'E' that was chiselled into the front of the temple, under the architrave and between the columns. It was the letter that assumed priority with the god, attaining the rank of a sacred offering. It hung over the head of anyone entering Apollo's inner sanctum. Was it in welcome, or a warning, or some kind of cryptic magical sign? Plutarch is puzzled by the meaning of the Delphic E.

Plutarch offers seven different speculative interpretations, several of which are beguiling. One of his suppositions is that the E represented the phonetic transcription of the Greek word *ei* — it might likewise be read as an emphatic contraction of the same two letters. Furthermore, the letter E, as a word, is spelt 'ei'.

Ei may itself be read in different ways. It translates, one way, as 'if'. The signal might then be to supplicants, an instruction, as they entered the temple, that all questions addressed to the Oracle should be phrased in 'if' terms — for example, '*If* I were to do x, would y or z be the consequences?' The Delphians themselves, in Plutarch's time, assumed this meaning.[7]

One modern scholar suggests that the intended meaning takes *ei* as an imperative form of the verb *eîmi*, 'I shall go'. It then commands the supplicant, 'You, go!'[8] If so, does this mean, 'Go on!' — that is, continue, enter inside, a signal of welcome? Or does it rather warn mortals: 'Go!', 'Leave while you still can!', 'You don't want to know the future; it won't do you any good!' 'Retreat in peaceful ignorance!'

Plutarch favours the interpretation that *Ei* means 'you are', another possible translation — the second-person singular, present-tense form of the verb 'to be'. The context is the words, 'Know thyself!' chiselled into the front of the temple, a form of welcome, and admonition. The god speaks to each one of us directly, as we approach him, with these words. We, in our turn, reply to him, in awe and reverence, 'You are', or 'You are the one.' The temple cues the form of address and homage to be used by the visitor. Plutarch puts it that acknowledgement of the god's eternal being, and majesty is the mortal antithesis to the warning, *Know thyself*.[9] The E is a 'Hail' to the divinity, in praise and devotion, one with unusually specific content.

But would the temple cue the supplicant in this manner? I have my doubts. This divinity does not stoop so low, down to the level of the ignorant visitor. It seems more plausible to me that E is the temple's own homage to Apollo. It stands as a cryptic way of asserting that Apollo is *being*. It proclaims that any pitiable mortal who enters here, enters the temple of existence. Delphi is the sacred site of *being*. E is Apollo's signature.

This reading finds support in a work by the most intelligent of all Western painters, Nicolas Poussin — 'the greatest of men' in his field. Poussin knew Plutarch's works well. In his 1647 version of *Ordination*, one of his second series of *Seven Sacraments*, now in Edinburgh, a magisterial Jesus stands in the centre, holding aloft a gold key in his left hand, and pointing down with a black key in his right. Peter kneels before him — it is clear from the gestures that, in a counter to orthodoxy, his path will be downwards (but that is another story). Behind Jesus is a massive, freestanding rectilinear pillar, with a large capital E carved into its capital. The E is the symbolic authority governing the scene. John, the beloved follower, stands opposite Jesus with head back, looking up, his arms apart and palms exposed forwards, open to the truth. His line of sight is directly at the E, through the gold key and Jesus's left index finger, which points upwards. John, in his own Life of Jesus, written much later, will stress that the Master's central message is about *being*, that the only important thing to know is, as Jesus puts it, 'I am'.[10] *I am* and *You are*.

'Know thyself!' is opaque, in that there are different types of knowledge. The dictum might refer to biographical facts, like a person's parentage, which is what Oedipus assumed. Or, as it would more likely be read today, it directs individuals to know their traits, their talents and strengths; what kind of work they are chosen to do; and what kind of person they are most suited to marry, or form close friendship with. The E, however, cuts across all of this, signalling that what is to be known is the essential self, the sacred inner being. *Who are you, Oedipus?*

The Karyatids find their Delphic self in three forms. There is firstly, and most obviously, the prophetess housed in the centre of Apollo's Temple — the Pythia. She was named after the monstrous snake-dragon that had lived in a cave here, the giant python killed by Apollo. In fact, the place was called Pytho until the fifth-century BC, when it slowly became 'Delphi'; in *Oedipus the King*, written around 426 BC, the reference is still to Pytho.

There is little detail in ancient sources as to the nature of the prophetess. Perhaps, because she was so well known, it was unnecessary to report the familiar. What we can piece together is that she was appointed for life; she was chosen from the local population of Delphi; and her utterances were in prose and verse, although in the latter case probably pithy local phrasing rather than high poetry. She was, in most periods, a virgin. One story has it that a young virgin Pythia was raped by a supplicant, a desecration that induced the town to appoint only women over the age of fifty.

Early sources report her wildly hallucinating, in manic trances fed by intoxicating vapours coming out of the ground. There is reference to a *chasma gēs* (a cleft into the earth) in the heart of the temple, out of which the sacred vapours rose. The *Homeric Hymn to Hermes* refers to her drunk on sweet honey, prophesying.[11] Plutarch, much later, writes that hardly had the Pythia sat down than a mania seized her. The Pythia was served by two priests, two prophets, and five *Hesioi*, or temple bureaucrats.[12] Some modern scholars dispute the Dionysian mania, suggesting that she rather spoke coherently, directly to the enquirer; priests were present, but only played a minor attendant role.[13]

Supplicants — whether a person or a group seeking the Oracle's pronouncement — would have passed through a lengthy and expensive process before gaining access to the Pythia. The process included paying a fee to Delphi and carrying out two complicated ritual sacrifices, which, in their turn, were costly. Early sources report the Oracle sitting on only one day a year; later, on one day, or sequence of days, per month. The pilgrimage to Delphi must have entailed much gruelling, nervous, expectant waiting.

Let us accompany the supplicants when the appointment date finally arrived. They would have walked up the ramp at the front of Apollo's Temple, and entered under the E, between two columns, into the *pronaos*, or foyer. They would then have been escorted through an open portal into the main part of the temple, the *megaron*, which was a vast, long hall enclosed on all sides by high walls, themselves decorated with painted scenes. Two lines of eight columns ran the length of the hall, in effect dividing it into three long naves.

Behind the row of columns on the supplicants' right was the sanctuary to Poseidon. The sea god was probably celebrated here because he had been the husband of Gaia, the goddess of the earth, and source of the *chasma gēs*. Poseidon was lord of the sanctuary in its archaic Pytho days, before Apollo took over.

There was a second sanctuary inside the *megaron*, but we do not know where exactly. It was the Pythia's own domain, perfumed with oil, inside which burned a perpetual flame, fed by laurel branches. The laurel was sacred to Apollo — from the legend that had him pursuing Daphne, who, in order to escape seduction, had herself turned into a laurel tree. Plutarch reports that surveillance of this sanctuary was restricted to chaste women, in effect the vestal virgins of Delphi.[14] Symbolically, Apollo, the civilised god, not given to rancour, enshrined the elusive and chaste nymph, Daphne, as his Delphic prophetess. He sublimated his frustrated desire into her oracular chant, in effect making her his voice. She acted like his ventriloquist doll.

There were four statues inside the *megaron*. Two represented the *Moirai* — the Fates. Plutarch is puzzled as to why there are only two Fates in Delphi, not the usual three. (The three Fates had different tasks: one spun the thread of each individual's life, one measured out its length, and one cut it when time was up.) The two other statues inside the *megaron* were of Zeus and Apollo — the latter known as Apollo *Moiragetēs*, 'conductor of the Fates'.

The supplicants, once having been escorted to the rear of the *megaron*, would have been led down a few steps into the secluded place of consultation. There, from an isolated corner, perhaps through columns, they would have caught their first sight of the Pythia. One can imagine their excitement, spiced with fear and wonder. (Some sources suggest she was concealed behind a curtain from supplicants.)

The prophetess of Delphi, the most famous woman in the world at the time, although anonymous, sat on a bronze tripod, three to four feet high, with her feet off the ground. (A tripod in ancient Greece was a three-legged stand that would normally hold a cauldron for heating water over a fire.) Early that same morning, the Pythia would have prepared herself by bathing in the sacred waters of the Kastalian spring, situated near the entrance to the Oracle complex, just down the road towards Thebes. The spring still flows today.

The *omphalos* stone rested close by the Pythia in the inner sanctum. One legend held it to have fallen to earth as a sign that Delphi was the centre of the world. *Omphalos* in Greek means 'navel', and the stone was a sign from Zeus that Delphi was the navel of the earth. Legend also held that it was the stone which

Zeus's mother, Rhea, disguised in swaddling clothes so that her husband, Chronos, would swallow it, thinking it to be the baby Zeus. Chronos later vomited the stone up, and Zeus placed it at Delphi. In short, the mythological genesis of Delphi is obscure and complex, with both Apollo and Zeus involved. This fits for a place where such an intensity of religious force, both upper-worldly and under-worldly, is concentrated

A Hellenistic or Roman copy of the *Omphalos* stone can be seen today in the Delphi Museum, looking like a giant acorn, with a patterning network of ropes carved across its surface. At the world's navel the net of fate encloses everything that is.

The Pythia kept laurel close beside her — whether branches or a living tree, we do not know. Also, in this small room, called the *adyton*, was a gold statue of Apollo. There may have been a fountain, with sacred water piped from the Kastalian Spring for the Pythia to drink. And, to compound the profusion and intensity of sacred objects, there was, by the fourth-century BC, the tomb of the god Dionysus. (Dionysus also appeared on the west pediment of Apollo's temple when it was rebuilt in the fourth century.[15])

At some point in the proceedings, she burned bay leaves and barley meal on an altar. And she wore a bay-leaf crown and held a bay sprig in her hand, shaking it on occasion.[16] Some scholars assume her to be more Dionysian, chewing bay leaves, with wild utterances interpreted by her priests, intoxicated on vapours coming from a fissure in the ground. Georges Roux stresses her double inspiration: the earthly vapour coming out of the ground in the *adyton*, and the heavenly *theion pneuma*, the godly pneuma of Apollo, breathing through her.[17]

What sort of questions was she asked? We have recorded evidence of 248 prophecies, which can be divided between legendary (176) and historical ones (72). The legendary prophecies are of more interest than the ones that can claim some historical veracity, given that the Oracle was so steeped in exotic mystery, fabulous and obscure ritual, and extravagant legend, and was situated in a remote site on a sacred mountain, a site which packed in a cornucopia of wealth and art. If there is any location in the history of the West where John Ford's dictum holds true, it is here at Delphi: 'When the legend becomes fact, print the legend.'

A small minority of oracular pronouncements referred to the future: some were clear; and some were ambiguous or conditioned. Most pronouncements were to do with religious questions, about sacrifices, religious laws and customs, and founding a cult. Public political questions were also put, on such matters as rulership, legislation, and colony founding. Individuals, such as Oedipus, also visited the Oracle with domestic questions about birth, marriage, death, career, and rewards.[18]

These facts, however, are rather beside the point. It is inconceivable that the supplicants saw coolly and clearly what confronted them in the *adyton*, charged as they were with the suspense that must have built up on the long and difficult journey to reach Delphi, followed by an often extreme wait, during which they could not be sure that they would ever gain admittance. Overwhelmed by the euphoria and dread induced by the ritual and the surrounds, their minds dazed by the Pythia's repute (dwarfing any celebrity aura today), they now finally stood inside the navel of the earth, in the presence of the divine power that could, in an instant, ruin their lives.

Imagine the fear of what they were about to hear. Would their nightmares be spoken out as divine truth? Or would something even worse than a nightmare be uttered in this confined chamber in the bowels of Apollo's Temple — a horror beyond bearable comprehension, as happened with Oedipus? The woman seated in front of them, her feet dangling free from the ground, unearthed, like some radiated apparition surrounded by her attributes of magic potency, breathing in the *pneuma* of the god, sang out her encrypted visions, foretelling, Kassandra-like, their future. Her chant spelled out the implacability of fate. She herself was the third *Moirai*, the last of the Fates.

The second manifestation of the Karyatid presence in Delphi is the archetypal human story determined from here. Oedipus lives completely under the shadow of prophetic Apollo and his three *Moirai*. His is a story obsessed by Necessity: a supremely confident and intelligent man yoked to his destiny, writhing to set himself free, and failing. When he descended into the *adyton*, the voice intoning through the vapours and the smoke must have sounded to him like a bell tolling his doom.

Oedipus's story is a disquisition on knowledge. His destiny is encrypted in his name. Its surface meaning is literal: *oîdos-pous*, meaning swollen-foot. The baby whose ankle tendons had been pierced, its feet tethered, had swollen feet. But *oîda* also means 'I know'. Oedipus is 'knowing foot'.

Oedipus's first recorded encounter, after continuing on towards Thebes from the parricidal three-ways junction, is with the Sphinx. She is the dark supernatural presence in the story: a monster with a woman's head, a lioness's body, a serpent's tail, and an eagle's wings. She dwelt by the road near Thebes, posing to everyone who passed by the riddle taught her by the Muses: 'Which being has four feet in the morning, two at noon, and three in the evening?' When those challenged failed to answer, she throttled them, and devoured them on the spot.[19] Laius, when he encountered his grown-up son, had been on his way to Delphi to ask the Oracle how he could rid Thebes of the curse of the Sphinx. Sophocles refers to her variously as the 'hook-taloned maid of the riddling speech' and 'rhapsode's dog'. The latter reference is to her being a servant of Apollo — she who sings his tune. The Sphinx is the voice of Apollo down on the profane earthly plane.

Oedipus meets her on the road to Thebes. He answers the riddle correctly: 'humans', from the baby crawling on all fours, to the adult walking in the noontime of life, to the old man limping along with the help of a walking-stick. In fact, the riddle plays on 'feet' — four, two, three. One might translate four as swollen-two, and three as two propped up by a blind man's stick. The subject of the riddle narrows down to Oedipus himself, the quintessential man.

The Sphinx is mortified that her mystery has been penetrated, and kills herself. It turns out, though, that her job is done, for she has carried out Apollo's assignment. She has rooted Oedipus in Thebes; trapped him in the net of his fate. He is initiated as the man of knowledge — he who solves riddles that no other humans can.

On that road of destiny, overshadowed by a prophecy of what will inevitably be, all wayfarers are warned by the story to beware of the encounter with the hook-taloned maid. She is both monster and seductress. Jean-Dominique Ingres painted her in 1808 flirting with Oedipus.[20] She gazes intently straight down into his eyes, moving her lioness's paw forward to tap him playfully, erotically, her serpent's tail flicking excitedly. She thrusts her large, firm, naked breasts at him. The virile young man cannot resist. However, in Ingres' portrayal, Oedipus is intoxicated yet retains his composure;

INGRES: OEDIPUS AND THE SPHINX, 1808

true to his nature, he reacts in a knowing, controlled, civilised manner. Knowing-foot coaxes the Sphinx out of her cave by the roadside, looking her straight in the eye, unflinchingly, beckoning her with his own hooked finger. He woos her fatally with his wit.

But why does she have to die? This is a most strange encounter. Her attributes and her reputation suggest that she possesses great supernatural powers and some kind of immortal malevolence. Also, she is the agent of Apollo. The answer must be that the mystery of the riddling speech is her life-blood, her essence. Once Oedipus has penetrated that and, in effect, stolen it, she withers away. She has lost who she is.

A further twist is hereby added to the story. Oedipus is more than the most intelligent of men: he is the one chosen to unlock the mystery. He does so without knowing what he is doing; just as he killed his father without knowing what he was doing; just as he will marry his mother without knowing what he is doing. He does understand the surface facts: he solved the riddle, and the Sphinx died. What he does not realise is that he is driven by a powerfully unconscious knowing. He is like a sleepwalker who treads a very carefully mapped-out path, utterly blind to where he is going, and why.

Encounters with three daimonic female personages govern Oedipus's journey: the first is the Delphic Pythia; the second is the monster under the place where the three ways meet; the third is the Sphinx. All three are linked to Apollo.

After the defeat of the Sphinx, the Thebans reward their saviour who has rescued them from death. They title him 'the greatest of men', and make him their new king, marrying him to the old queen. Years pass. The signs are that Oedipus is a good king and a good father — he has four children with Jokasta. Then plague strikes

Thebes: death returns. In desperation, the king sends for advice from the Delphic Oracle. He is told that the pestilence will not abate until the killers of the old king are found and banished.

The true pursuit of knowledge begins. Oedipus calls the prophet Teiresias, who tells him that he himself is the cause of the pollution befouling the city. Oedipus, whose one character flaw is a short temper, angrily abuses the prophet as a primitive charlatan dependent on bird signs: where was he when the riddle of the Sphinx needed solving? *I, Oedipus, am the man who, by my wit alone, can see into dark secrets; I have proved myself.* And, given the enormity, the potency, of his own victory over the primeval riddling monster, it is little wonder that he scorns Teiresias.

But the hook-talons have him in the grip of the true riddle, not the abstract one about men in general. 'Know thyself, Oedipus!' It slowly dawns on Oedipus that the Oracle was right. In recognition of the abomination of what he has done — especially in fathering four children with his own mother — he blinds and exiles himself. This is the surface horror of his life. Who would want to be him?

Yet, reverberating in the depths of the story is a deeper shame, one he cannot bear to look on. In his pride, in his foolish overconfidence, he imagined he could outwit his destiny. His crime has been against *sōphrosunē*. His uncontrolled anger is trivial next to his excessive pride. Now he can sense the god of Delphi up there, not so far away, looking down on him from his mountain site, and smiling in sad mockery at this pitiful human specimen — at him, Oedipus, who thought he was the greatest of men.

Oedipus does become great, but in a quite different way. He becomes the paradigm for what it is to be human in the new Greek world of Athena and Apollo. It is the paradigm that will govern the West's view of the human essence. Once upon a time, Oedipus had been admired as a man of sharp wit and rational knowledge: as a king, as a father, and as a confident, self-determining individual. The modern Western world would admire him in precisely the same way, for precisely the same things. But that past self is now eclipsed, superseded. 'Know thyself' takes another fork in the road.

Rather, the story reveals Oedipus, by the end, as the man who is inwardly driven to find out the truth about himself; and, when he does so, the one who is able to face it, full on, and take responsibility into his own hands for the consequences. At no point does he shirk, evade, or retreat: his denial to Teiresias is momentary; above all, when the truth is revealed, he does not take the easier way out, like his mother, Jokasta, who kills herself. He blinds himself; he banishes himself to live out the rest of his life alone on the hillside where he had been put out as a baby to die. He gives himself time to digest what he has done — many years, maybe even decades. He sets about learning to live with who he is. The coming time will be bitter, cold, and lonely. He will be hounded by thoughts of his poor children, and especially his beloved daughters, and how impossible it will be for them to fashion any normal life, given the horrible burden of their origins.

Yet it is possible — and here is his triumph — that he will come to find himself in harmony with his terrible fate. It is possible that he will come to find himself in tune with the Delphic god who has overseen it all. He can finally reply to Teiresias's opening assertion, 'Woe, woe, to know is terrible.' If the knowledge is of the Delphic E, all may be well and fair. Oedipus, whose unwitting quest is for the *mystery* — the mystery that all humans must encounter if they are to live — finds it in the E.

The third Karyatid presence in Delphi is that of Athena herself. Her penetrating eye rests on the scene.

Apollo's Temple is massive and grand; one can still sense this today. It is almost overbearing in proportion to the rest of the Oracle's domain. Looking out from it, the visitor makes out the second sacred site at Delphi, a kilometre away and below. There are another series of ruins, visually highlighted by the columns of the Tholos rotunda. Beyond the Tholos, at the back of this secondary site, is a temple of Athena.

Athena's Temple is intimate, nestling quietly in an olive grove, discreet, almost hidden. Built around 500 BC, it was of medium size — 27m by 13m, or 12 columns by 6 columns. This temple was the best preserved on the entire Delphi site, before it was flattened by an earthquake in 1905. There is a soft enchantment to the mood in its vicinity, calming, breathing a kind of serenity that inclines the visitor to pause, slow down, and ease into the composure of just being here. The olive trees seem to have preserved some of their ancient sacred aura — their place is a sanctuary. Olympia shares some of this arcadian calm. Looking up from Athena's modest corner, Apollo's domain spreads across the far hillside; from this perspective, not at all grandiose (see p. 148).

Why was Athena given such a major presence in Apollo's shrine? One legend attributes it to Apollo's gratitude for her help in killing the Pytho.[21] The suggestion is that Apollo was not up to the challenge on his own. In his ephebe disposition, there is something less than fully masculine about him; some weakness that would feel under greatest challenge in taking on a demonic female force — one with the attributes of a giant python that circles its enveloping coils around the victim and squeezes to death, and then devours the corpse. The Sphinx has some of these Pytho attributes.

Apollo as Sun God was explicitly separated from the dark lunar forces linked with his sister, Artemis. So he sought the aid of Athena. Was it her craftiness, her predominant capacity among the gods for brilliant strategy, which he sought? Or was it her uncompromising warrior self, and her intimate knowledge of Karyatid forces, that made her uniquely suited to outsmarting primitive female malevolence slithering silently out of a dark crevice in the black cave?

The two temples share an affinity with this legend. There is a heavy, almost lumbering clumsiness to Apollo's Temple in Delphi. It has none of the light elegant vitality of the Parthenon. It is over-masculine, suggestive in modern psychological terminology of 'protest masculinity': it over-stresses what it fears it lacks. By contrast, there is a calm serenity in Athena's corner. Her domain here is more modest, more feminine, than her usual self. The grey-eyed merciless warrior is in hibernation. She is at ease. I suspect that the ambience results from recognition that what might have turned into a contest between Apollo and herself has been resolved, and without any distress. (Things were not always so harmonious between them. They backed opposing sides in the Trojan War, with Apollo hating, and managing to kill, her protégé, Achilles — a subject to which I shall turn in the next chapter.)

The two gods share attributes. They are representatives of the new order on Olympus, with a driving ambition to civilise humanity. They are the two champions of *sōphrosunē*. Both are, in essence, truth gods. Apollo presides over its prophetic, fatalistic mode; Athena is herself the source of both rational Parthenon intelligence and deep Karyatid wisdom. The overlap continues in the persona of Kassandra, who gained her prophetic powers as a gift from Apollo, in a failed attempt to seduce her. Kassandra has

Karyatid gravity, linking her with Athena. Finally, both Apollo and Athena are patrons of poetry, song, and other arts — the means through which gifted humans voice the unconscious truths, and thereby come to know them.

Athena and Apollo are half-sister and half-brother. Zeus is their common father. It is they who inherit the father's kingdom, peacefully, without deposing him. There is fraternity here, and shared goals. In Delphi, it is as if the sister benevolently gazes up over her brother's domain, wishing it well, for she may draw on deeper and broader resources. She is respectful of his power to know the future, his command of the Fates, and his generosity to humans in communicating what will be to those who know how to listen. Oedipus is his human hero, and reflection — just as she champions Achilles and Odysseus.

The spatial orchestration between Apollo and Athena here is the work of subtle genius. Delphi engages us with its range of balances, all working together to create the whole. The harmony between the two gods is the crux. Whoever chose these sites and laid them out knew what they were doing. Here, the human is working in homage to two divine orders, and siting its devotion in a remote and grand expanse of nature.

Delphi has another element: the bronze, life-sized sculpture of the Charioteer, housed today in the Museum. A few decades older than the Parthenon, it is its counterpart. Here is the Parthenon in human form.

In him, humanity is stripped back to the essence of existing, standing, alert in its vocation, in its worldly role. This is a young

DELPHI CHARIOTEER, C 470 BC

man, in whom details of character and life-path are unknown and of little consequence. He is the idealised human form — sculptural, defined by clean, simple lines rather than by any detailing. We know him less by his facial expression than by his long robe (the *chiton*), whose fluted folds impose a vertical purity. The young man is in a timeless, worldly trance, gazing out and beyond, as if absorbed in a Zen-like meditation. In him, the divine predominates, so the fact that one of his arms is missing is hardly to be noticed. He articulates the serene poise of *virtue transcendent*, in the particular form of the archetypal human individual standing alone in the world.

Polyzalos, one of the Deinomenid tyrants of Syracuse, the Greek colony in Sicily, entered a chariot in the Pythian Games of 478 or 474 BC, and won. In order to celebrate, and to perpetuate the memory of the victory, he had a bronze group sculpted. It included a charioteer, a chariot, and two separate horses with their grooms. A number of fragments apart from the charioteer have survived. The whole was dedicated to Apollo, according to a partly preserved inscription on the pedestal.[22]

The Charioteer is ephebe-like, a human counterpart to the youthful Apollo. He is hardly more than a boy, fresh-faced, with no hint of a beard, his features almost feminine, adorned with delicate curls. He shows the famous classical Greek profile: a long, straight nose, running up into the forehead with hardly any bridge to interrupt its line; fullish lips; and a rounded, slightly protruding chin (see p. 143). His eyes are made from white enamel, with black, inset stones for the pupils. The restrained elegance is highlighted by his small, finely sculpted feet.

He is an athlete, a winner at the Pythian Games — an achievement more celebrated in his time than Olympic gold-medal success is today. Not only were works of art commissioned to immortalise the victor, but the poet Pindar wrote odes to the champions, many of which have come down to us. In Perikles' time, huge purses were paid to victors at the Panathenian Games — in one case, 140 large jars, or amphoras, of sacred oil to the winner of the two-horse chariot race.[23] It is telling that the two finest works of sculpture to have survived from ancient Greece both represent athletes: the Charioteer, and the bronze javelin-thrower, sometimes called the Zeus of Artemisium, housed today in the Athens Museum (see p. 84). These two figures are unsurpassed by the greatest of Italian Renaissance sculpture.

The Charioteer is illustrative of the Greek athletic ideal, that of *eurythmia*: beautiful rhythm. His athletic excellence results from a highly trained mind and body working in harmony. The performance depends on intense focus on the specific task at hand — a mental poise in which all normal fears, anxieties, and superfluous thoughts are banished, leaving the mind in a state of composure akin to meditation. He then drives his chariot as if, to use a recurring Homeric metaphor, a god breathes through him. He is inspired. He is larger than his normal everyday self. In the chariot race, he achieves a moment of grace — pagan grace. He is an exemplar of athletic religion, with chariot-driving being his mode of prayer. He embodies *virtue transcendent*, and as such is the Delphic equivalent of the Parthenon.

The chariot is his life. He steers it with masterly skill — the reins held lightly, deftly tugged to tame the snorting fury of his galloping horses, harnessing their power. His ride is swift, negotiating the tight bend of the Delphi stadium, and the uneven track, at precipitous speeds. He prevails. He does more than prevail; he becomes a shining beacon of how to live. It is little wonder, then, that what he was — the legend — is celebrated, and for eternity, in bronze poetry.

The Charioteer has no guile. No Karyatid enigma intrudes on his innocence. In fact, he is the polar opposite in human form of the six dark maidens. In Delphi, the Charioteer complements Oedipus, and together they represent the full range of the human story, each standing at either extreme of a continuum. We humans all live on that continuum, our natures and what we encounter woven from elements of both these archetypal figures.

The Charioteer is the third of the big presences in Delphi. There is Apollo, manifest in his sanctuary, his power illustrated through the prophecies of the Pythia; and elaborated in the saga of Oedipus. There is Athena. And there is the life-size bronze image of beautiful rhythm. Together, these three contribute to the overarching Delphic presence, that of the site itself.

It is a miracle that the Charioteer exists today. Why did this masterpiece, rather than the thousands of lesser works, survive the ravages of pillage, earthquake, and time — to be unearthed by French archaeologists a century ago? It is like the parallel miracle of the Delphi landscaping, which must have slowly emerged over many generations, and not from the blueprint of one master designer. It is as if a presiding divinity had a hand in instating, then preserving, paradigms of the sacred in Delphi. Some places on the earth seem to be blessed.

ZEUS OF ARTEMISIUM

FOUR

HOMER

The third foundation site is Troy. At the *mythos* level, as I read it, the ancient Greek story begins in Troy, with Homer. As Walter Otto puts it, 'The Homeric poems are the greatest Greek monuments.'[1]

Today, we visitors to the ancient Greek world arrive first in Athens, and then work backwards in time. This is true literally, at the tourist level, with the common entry-point to the country being Athens airport, except for those travelling directly to the islands. Also, it is usually true in terms of what the visitor knows, and finds intriguing about classical Greece. Stories of the Trojan War, Odysseus's adventures, familiar myths, Olympia, and fascination with the Delphic Oracle may all play a role in arousing our curiosity. Yet, for most, it is the glory of fifth-century Athens that is the centre of the attraction. That glory draws on the Parthenon and philosophy; sculpture in marble and bronze; law and democracy; Marathon and Salamis; the Periklean Empire and mathematics;

and, above all, the city itself, the polis, as the founding jewel of Western civilisation.

Nevertheless, reading the story in reverse, as I have done in this book, also makes sense, starting with the fifth-century Athenians and their Acropolis. Athens sets up the parameters that guide us as we look further back in time — first to Delphi, and then to Homer. It is as if there is a constantly ebbing and flowing tide of *mythos* consciousness, from Troy to Delphi to the Acropolis, from the Acropolis back to Delphi, and on further back to Troy. There is a connection here with the surprising fact that the Greek language gets more difficult as one proceeds backwards chronologically from, say, Plato to Aeschylus to Homer.

Ancient Troy is quite different from the other two sites, in coming down to us almost entirely as a place of the mind. Modern archaeologists have found the physical site, and partially excavated it, discovering something like nine cities built one on top of each other — each rebuilding replacing its predecessor, destroyed in turn by earthquakes, wars, or other disasters. There are negligible remains from the seventh city, the one most likely to have been King Priam's fortress, destroyed by the Greeks at the end of the Trojan War. That war is assumed to have taken place around 1200 BC, towards the end of the Mycenaean empire. Moreover, over three millennia of alluvial silting have changed the landscape around Troy — and especially the course of the rivers and the coastline, filling in the large bay that the invading ancient Greeks used as a natural harbour.

Scholars, in the main, today believe that Homer composed the *Iliad* in the late eighth century, maybe a little earlier than 700 BC.[2] If so, there is a five-hundred-year chasm separating the events from the epic, probably filled with oral transmission of stories of many of the episodes. This is the period of the dark ages that descended on Greece and Crete between 1200 BC and 800 BC — a period of reversion to prehistoric illiteracy, in which very little material culture, from buildings to clay figures, was produced. What happened during these four centuries remains unknown.[3]

About Homer himself, little is sure. He was possibly an Asiatic Greek, born on or near the coast of Asia Minor — the west, Aegean coast of modern Turkey. The island of Chios and the town of Smyrna have the strongest claims on him.

Once the *mythos* is carried by a virtuoso human creation, the text becomes the sacred site, and the geographical location is demoted to that of a subsidiary appendage. In the history of the West, this is nowhere truer than with Homer: the *Iliad* is the foundational Western story; in chronology, the first, the oldest. In a similar way, the Biblical sites, notably Jerusalem and the Sea of Galilee, are superseded by the written narratives of the Life of Jesus, led by Mark.

A physical site may, nevertheless, anchor a text, providing it with spatial projection. There are different modes. In the case of the Acropolis in Athens, the two temples serve as the artworks that transmit the story. They are, in effect, the texts; yet, at the same time, these texts are dependent on their physical location. With Delphi, the site predominates, one mapped out and developed by humans: it is supplemented by two great artistic creations, Sophocles' drama *Oedipus the King*, and the bronze Charioteer.

Troy is at the other polar extreme from Delphi: the physical site is insignificant. We know Troy as imagined and projected by Homer. And the actual site of most of the action in the *Iliad* is not as it was. The terrain has changed, from the coastal camp near where the Greek ships were beached, to the plains between there and the city, including the River Skamandros, across which the fighting took place.

If Troy is a place largely of the mind, we are faced with the question of what cultural status works of art may claim. A parallel from today may help with clarification. To my mind, the greatest modern reworking of Homer's epic has been John Ford's masterpiece *The Searchers*. This film was shot amidst the spectacular rock formations of Monument Valley, on the border of Utah and Arizona. Monument Valley is the same today is it was in 1955 when Ford worked on location there. Its panoramas are breathtaking, especially when navigated on horseback — which I did in 2007. Yet, I was surprised, in reflecting afterwards on the experience of being there, to realise that the mythic force of the actual Monument Valley was pale compared with what moves me when engrossed in the film, the screen landscape forming the backdrop to darkly sublime human tragedy. The *mythos*, articulated by the great human imagination, transforms the landscape.

Delphi spawns one of the three great Greek trials of meaning — that of Oedipus. The *Iliad* is responsible for the other two — itself, and Aeschylus's *Agamemnon*. The singular and primal genius of Homer's epic was such that fifth-century Athenians took it as what we would call their Bible. In fact, Homer takes up the disparate and chaotic threads of Greek mythology, and integrates them into his narrative, providing a highly charged, coherent *mythos*. Homer scripts the archetype that will govern much of what is to come, first in the classical Greek world, and then throughout the West. Alexander the Great always slept with a copy of the *Iliad* under his pillow. Pausanias records that the ancient Olympic Games were opened with a ritual mourning for Homeric Achilles.[4]

Finally, in this preamble, on a journey in search of *archē*, in quest of the genesis, it is significant that Homer, the Delphic Oracle, and the Olympic Games all date to the eighth century BC. And all were pan-Hellenic — that is, universal. It is the century following the four-hundred-year dark ages that sees the birth of ancient Greek culture.

The *Iliad* is broken into twenty-four books. The story is Achilles, even though, for the first nineteen of them, he remains mainly a shadowy presence in the background, doing very little. Achilles broods angrily, camped near his ships, simmering with petulant outrage, refusing to enter the fighting, driven unrelentingly by pride over his wounded dignity. His behaviour is childish, pre-cultural. He represents the embryonic human, in the form of a spoilt brat, before he enters through the gates of culture.

Homer's opening lines warn the reader, or listener, not to be fooled by surface appearances. With portentous gravity, they prefigure what is to come:

> Sing, goddess, the anger of Peleus' son Achilleus,
> and its devastation ...

The thread that strings the story to follow is anger, that of Achilles: it will drive the events that matter. Moreover, lest the audience takes what it is to hear lightly, the story has pre-eminent authority — its source is the goddess. It is *extra-ordinary*. This is not some ephemeral tale, told by a mortal idiot, 'full of sound and fury, signifying nothing'[5]. It is sacred story, casting its calibrating net over the human condition, interpreting what is, and stipulating what ought to be.

The two cultural orders, of the Parthenon and of the Karyatids, will play out in sequence and then come together, fusing at the climax of the *Iliad*.

The Shining order is evoked in two ways. First, there is the fighting, up until Book 16, when Patroklos enters the fray and the mood darkens. Homer describes the earlier battles with a lyrical quality, as men sweep and surge over the plain, caught up in their hymns to heroism and glory. It is like sport. The exemplary individual is the Greek warrior Diomedes. Through his excellence in battle, he represents *virtue transcendent*. The Trojans assume that some god possesses him, or fights beside him; for his part, Homer ascribes pure and powerful forces of nature to him, through the use of simile:

> [H]e went storming up the plain like a winter-swollen
> river in spate that scatters the dikes in its running current,
> one that the strong-compacted dikes can contain no longer
> neither the mounded banks of the blossoming vineyards hold it
> rising suddenly as Zeus' rain makes heavy the water
> and many lovely works of the young men crumble beneath it.
> Like these the massed battalions of the Trojans were scattered
> by Tydeus' son, and many as they were could not stand against
> him.[6]

The second manifestation of *virtue transcendent* is represented by Achilles' companion, Patroklos. He has a quality of charming gentleness that transcends the brutality of war. Briseis, the slave mistress of Achilles, grieves over the corpse of Patroklos, taking it in her arms, likening him to her slain husband: 'I weep your death without ceasing. You were always kind.'[7] Even Achilles' horses, given to him by the gods, stand back from the battle and shed tears at the death of Patroklos. Likewise, the Trojan hero Hektor is admired for his gentleness — Helen laments the fact, over his body, that he was the only one who was kind to her, and a friend.[8]

The *Iliad* switches cultural orders in Book 16. Its turning-point happens with gentle Patroklos entering battle wearing the armour of Achilles. In the heat of battle, even he gets carried away, 'in a huge blind fury, besotted'. Triumphal and sadistic blood-lust surges. The climax comes with him shamelessly mocking a Trojan he has just killed:

> The sharp stone hit him in the forehead
> and smashed both brows in on each other, nor could the bone
>   hold
> the rock, but his eyes fell out into the dust before him
> there at his feet, so that he vaulted to earth like a diver
> from the carefully wrought chariot, and the life left his bones.
>   Now
> you spoke in bitter mockery over him, rider Patroklos:
> 'See now, what a light man this is, how agile an acrobat.
> If only he were somewhere on the sea, where the fish swarm,
> he could fill the hunger of many men, by diving for oysters;
> he could go overboard from a boat even in rough weather
> the way he somersaults so light to the ground from his chariot
> now. So, to be sure, in Troy also they have their acrobats.'[9]

This is the first time that Homer addresses a character directly — 'rider Patroklos' — and it weights the moment with a woeful compassion for the kind and gentle one. Tragic foreboding accompanies the violation of *sōphrosunē*. This mocking, which is so out of character for Patroklos, spells his own doom. Even more, it signals the story's turn, and plunge into the dark. Zeus has just 'swept ghastly night far over the strong encounter'.

The same switch is prefigured in an early exchange between Hektor and his wife, Andromache, inside the Trojan Palace. Hektor foresees that Troy will fall, and his wife will be led off as a slave. He laments:

> But may I be dead and the piled earth hide me under before I hear
> you crying and know by this that they drag you captive.[10]

At which, he holds out his arms to take his baby son, but the son starts screaming at the aspect of his father. Hektor switches mood, laughs, tosses his son about in his arms, kisses him, and lets hopeful illusions buoy his spirits:

> Poor Andromache! Why does your heart sorrow so much for me?
> No man is going to hurl me to Hades, unless it is fated,
> but as for fate, I think that no man yet has escaped it.

Kind, family-loving Hektor, too, will get carried away in the heat of battle. After he kills Patroklos, he strips his armour and leaves the body naked. He then engages in a furious struggle with the Greeks to carry the corpse off as a trophy, with the intention of taking it back to Troy, decapitating it, then exhibiting the head on a stake, and feeding the body to the dogs.

Achilles, when he hears news of the death of Patroklos, is swamped in a mania of grief and rage. His first move is to show himself unarmed to the Trojan army. He stands by the ditch protecting the Greek ships. Athena is present. She encircles his head in a golden cloud, with a far-shining flame flaring up from it. His head blazing, Achilles bellows out three times with a great cry. Athena adds her own shout. The Trojans are terrified.

There is no lyricism voiced once Achilles enters the battle. He is so much the superior warrior. What was once a fair and sporting contest between equals gives way to rampaging and pitiless slaughter. The battle-scene turns ugly:

> So before great-hearted Achilleus the single-foot horses
> trampled alike dead men and shields, and the axle under
> the chariot was all splashed with blood and the rails which
> encircled
> the chariot struck by flying drops from the feet of the horses,
> from the running rims of the wheels. The son of Peleus was
> straining
> to win glory, his invincible hands splattered with bloody filth.[11]

Achilles in battle is like a terror-inducing monster out of the pre-Homeric era: the era typified by Herakles' labours in combat with the Nemean lion and the Lernaean hydra; with stags, bulls, and boars; and with the three-headed Cerberus. In the *Iliad*, the actual monsters are gone, replaced by the rampaging hero.[12] To further complicate this evolution, the hero does not brandish a shield bearing the image of a threatening beast, like the Medusa, but one illustrated with scenes of civilisation. The shield of Achilles presages the future, including his own immediate future.

Signs of bitter wisdom appear in the heat of battle. Achilles responds with calm and pitiless logic to Lykaon, a young and helpless son of Priam who grabs his knees, pleading for his life:

> So, friend, you die also. Why all this clamour about it?
> Patroklos also is dead, who was better by far than you are.
> Do you not see what a man I am, how huge, how splendid
> and born of a great father, and the mother who bore me
>   immortal?
> Yet even I have also my death and my strong destiny,
> and there shall be a dawn or an afternoon or a noontime
> when some man in the fighting will take the life from me also ...[13]

We have walked down the incline from the bright light of the Parthenon, and have entered the Erechtheion. This speech is brutish but deep. Achilles knows his fate; in fact, this was anticipated in Book 9, where he reflected on his own choice of two fates. Achilles recounted that it was decreed he could return home to live a long and happy life in obscurity, or remain at Troy, fight, win immortal glory, but die soon.

This choice was no choice, because such abstraction is mere spume blowing off the crashing breakers of destiny, taking no account of the passions and attachments that determine human behaviour. In truth, Achilles lingers in his camp on the beach in Troy, held there by some inner need, and then events take over. The Trojans triumph, reaching the Greek ships, which they are about to burn ... Patroklos joins the battle, and is killed. And so one step leads inevitably on to the next.

Achilles knows that his rampaging excess in battle will offend the gods. Like Patroklos, he is in 'a huge blind fury, besotted', but at the same time partly detached, and in this he is different. He knows that what he does will bring divine retribution, but he decides that

Patroklos is worth it. In fact, the river-god Skamandros almost succeeds in drowning him, for Achilles wrongs nature, too, by polluting its waters — filling the river with Trojan corpses.

The outrages climax in a scene after Achilles has killed Hektor, stripped his armour, and mutilated the body. He cuts holes in Hektor's ankles next to the tendons, strings ox-hide thong through the holes, and ties the body to the back of his chariot. He then drives past the citadel of Troy, under the eyes of its wailing inhabitants, dragging the blood-smeared corpse through the dirt, feet first, its long, flowing hair thickening with the dust. He then speeds off, drawing it behind his chariot back to the Greek camp, where he leaves it for dogs to feed on. There is no respect, and no pity here; only bitter mockery and contempt. This is Achilles the monster.

Achilles' fury is a form of excess that hotly scorns the law of balance. Homer's opening words make it clear that this is no passing tantrum; they instruct us that the narrative will centre on the anger of Achilles, and the devastation it brings about. What we witness is a violation of sacred order, to which the gods cannot turn a blind eye. Indeed, the gods will bring the arch-hero down by targeting the heel, the very spot he chose to begin his despoiling of Hektor's corpse.

Once Achilles has killed Hektor, the battle ends. The last two Books of the *Iliad* follow, both directed by funerals, those of Patroklos and Hektor. They portray Achilles the gentleman. In the first, he organises funeral games. He provides the prizes, runs the events, and judges them — not competing himself. He settles disputes when the Greek warriors become petty, squabbling over a result or a prize. In fact, he sets, by his own example, such a tone of courtesy, fair play, and generosity that the other warriors are shamed into acting more like him, better than their normal selves. Berserk, merciless, man-slaughtering Achilles becomes the finest of men.

His last act is to welcome the enemy king, Priam, into his tent. Priam has come secretly at night to plead for the return of his son's corpse. Priam drops to his knees; he reminds Achilles of his own father, describing himself as the most wretched of all fathers, for who has had to do what he now does? 'I put my lips to the hands of the man who has killed my children.' Both men then break down and weep together. Achilles stands and takes the old man by the hand, addressing him, 'Aged, magnificent sir.'

Achilles had exemplified the view that the highest end of human life is to display heroic excellence: *arēte*. This is precisely what Agamemnon insults at the start of the story. Achilles fights not primarily for booty or communal honour, but for glory: *kleos*. The Homeric picture of life after death was not appealing — the ghost or shade condemned to an eternity of tedium in the Hades underworld (this picture would later change, with Plato, for instance, developing a full theory of the immortality of the soul). Hence, the goal for the Homeric hero became to make the most of his mortal life by achieving immortal fame. This may explain why Apollo is especially hostile to Achilles, engineering his death. Gregory Nagy suggests that god and hero function as ritual antagonists.[14] The age of heroes is replacing the age of gods; it, in turn, will soon be replaced by the endless age of ordinary mortals. Apollo is fighting for his own order.[15]

Nagy argues that Achilles' name breaks down into *achos-laos*, with *achos* meaning 'grief', and *laos* 'host of fighting men'. Achilles is, by nature, like a teeming swarm of warriors housed in one body — or, rather, warrior demons. He is, equally, the man of constant sorrow. From the start, he broods in grief over his confiscated mistress, Briseis, and the insult by the king to his honour. After the death of Patroklos, the grief becomes permanent, 'for never again will an *achos* like this enter my heart while I am among the living.' The grief of Achilles makes him angry, and his anger leads to grief for the Greeks (or the Achaeans, as they are often called). His first grief separates him from his warrior brothers (the *laos*); his second grief reunites him with them. Nagy reads the collective name, the Achaeans, as also derived from *achos*: they are the people subjected to constant grief.[16] Achilles is the leader of those who suffer and grieve.

This reading is plausible so far as it goes; but it stops short of the crux to the story. It fails to take account of the metamorphosis in Achilles. The hero changes from the man of supreme *arēte* to one who has lost all interest in his own glory and excellence. The heroic warrior turns into the tragic gentleman.

A modern sensibility may be troubled by what lurks beneath the surface here. As an instructive parallel, it is hard for the 'civilised' mind to comprehend the Greek mythological figure of Silenus — the bloated, fat, drunken old lecher, who lurched around groping anyone of either sex he could get his hands on. Silenus was wise. But how, we might ask, could such a repulsive beast — one who indulged, without conscience, every lust and form of sadism — have gained wisdom? Worse, how could he be the one to gain unique insight into great and profound truths? Achilles is like Silenus, in that his own monstrous deeds on the field of battle somehow make him uniquely suited to becoming the man of supreme courtesy and compassion.

The Achilles equation puts it this way: suffer the most extreme grief, express the most extreme rage, and achieve the most sublime balance.

Achilles incarnates the cultural symbiosis of the Parthenon and the Karyatids. In him, the two cultural orders fuse. There is his excellence as a man acting in the world, as the exemplary warrior — he is the best of all men at what he does, at what he was born to do. His presence shines. Once upon a time, his life was simple and clear like that of Diomedes. But there is more to Achilles. He has always played music — the lyre, like Apollo — and he sings.[17] He can reflect on who he is and the life-path that has been mapped out for him. He gains vision; he leads; and he gives practical advice. He becomes kind.

Achilles has become *virtue transcendent*, in a more complete mode than the Parthenon. Like Athena herself, he has achieved a balance between Shining and dark saying. His is not an ethical condition; this man has irredeemably violated fundamental moral laws, for which he pays. Achilles becomes great in his detachment — from his victories, from his peerless prowess as a warrior, and from his glory. He is past caring about any such worldly brilliance. Tragic suffering drives him to a new engagement with courtesy, with civilised behaviour, and with the aged, magnificent Sir, his enemy, whose state moves him to tears of understanding. In a strange way, Priam becomes his new companion, replacing Patroklos.

Achilles is the one, with Priam, who is crushed by suffering when part of his old self dies, including the arrogant, pre-cultural brat self. In his case, the cause of woe is twofold: the loss of his bosom-friend, Patroklos, and the awareness of his own dark destiny — that his death is imminent, a death that he will bring upon himself by what he is about to do. He sees the *ainigma*, gaining the wisdom of Kassandra. And, in spite of all he knows, he is not turned to stone. It is he, on the field of battle, who leaves a wasteland of death in his outrageous wake: 'see what a man I am, how huge, how splendid'. His grandeur as a man is both monstrous and awesome.

The hands spattered with bloody filth are the same hands that King Priam will kiss.

So it is little wonder that Athena crowns his entry into battle by bestowing him with the Shining aura. Here speaks the judgement of truth. Achilles is her pre-eminent human disciple. His three great shouts announce that the big man is about to harness himself to Necessity. What peals forth, blazing across the battlefield, heard by Greek and Trojan alike, is his sublime golden brilliance, wedded to avenging, demonic rage, and weighted with *gravitas*. He is what it is to be a man.

The story of Achilles takes metaphysics, centred on the nature of being, to a higher level. The surface story has it that the hero is punished for excess — for his lack of control in battle, and for his sacrilegious abuse of Hektor's corpse. In both spheres, however, he is just doing what any other warrior, including Hektor himself, would do. The difference lies in Achilles' size. He is such a big man, so much the superior warrior, that when he enters the battle, things become unbalanced. It is no longer a sporting contest between near-equals, but one-sided mass slaughter. Achilles can hardly be blamed: he is merely being true to himself as the greatest warrior of them all. Homer's description of him as 'godlike' is, in part, an allusion to his superhuman force as a fighter. Yet Achilles *is* punished by the gods. By this stage in our interpretation of the *Iliad*, the nature of Achilles' crime — for which he must pay with his own death— has become unclear.

It seems that Achilles is punished simply for being who he is: the big man. The ultimate necessity, the ultimate fatedness, is to be born who you are. The pained words spoken to Lykaon, 'Do you not see what a man I am, how huge, how splendid', have, as their undertone, the rueful acknowledgement that his very being is a crime against nature. He is the glorious man who shines, the man who gains the favour of Athena. Perhaps he shines too much; perhaps his fury is too *daimonic*. He is, after all, the man whose nature drives him to clog the river with Trojan corpses, and whose shining terrifies all the other warriors, whether Greek or Trojan. For this, he must pay, and prodigiously. Great gifts come at great cost. There will be balance. The *Agamemnon* chorus learns this lesson, and prays:

> And the vaunt of high glory
> is bitterness; for God's thunderbolts
> crash on the towering mountains.
> Let me attain no envied wealth,
> let me not plunder cities ...'[18]

But the *Agamemnon* chorus is not entirely convincing in its preference for a quiet, obscure life without glory. The moral it draws is at odds with the Homeric ethos. Homer's metaphysical cue would send us along a different path. *Mythos* decrees that Achilles be projected as larger than life, the greatest of men, and metaphorically semi-divine. This is not principally in order to distinguish him from other, lesser mortals, but to glorify him as the ideal human. He is what every man should aspire to be.

It follows that every individual will be punished, whoever he or she is. Certainly, the bigger the man, the heavier the punishment, but that does not change the basic equation. Nor does Homer moralise here, in contrast with the Christian doctrine of 'original sin': we humans suffer not because we are fallen sinners, but because of the simple existential fact that we are not gods. Homer notes, sadly, that this is how things are. He points to the essence of tragedy, which is inherent in being born human. So he gifts to Achilles the quality of immense courtesy, and the charm of making music.

The trace that Achilles leaves behind at the end of the *Iliad* is like the look of the Karyatids, a grim warning to approaching humans to stay away. *If you want to be this great, beware!* But here is the dilemma facing all mortals: the alternative is unthinkable. The alternative would be to have no story, and no truth — to have no life. Roberto Calasso put it that the gods get bored with men who have no stories.[19]

Further, it is not just an issue of losing contact with the beyond, of turning the gods away, out of boredom with our craven human pettiness. The story of Achilles portrays an ideal of how to gain enough powerful composure so as not to be paralysed. Its message to all humans is to live knowing their fate, like seeing the shadow form of a creature of the deep moving beneath, blurred and opaque: *Strap yourself to that fate, and live in as much harmony with it as possible, respectfully.* Even foolish and unkindly Agamemnon manages to harness himself to his destined script (exactly the terms used by Aeschylus) when it is too late to avert his doom.[20] Karyatid gravity accompanies such a life; it may serve as protection from the Medusa. If there is no truth, however dark, with the power to turn the human subject to stone, he or she should be able to act and move with excellence and grace in the world. Then the goddess will accompany, shining with song.

Homer himself counterpoises Odysseus to Achilles. These two men incarnate competing ideal types of being human. The poet devotes his second work to telling the story of Odysseus on his journey home after the Trojan War. I don't intend here to enter the fruitless debate about whether the same man wrote the *Iliad* and the *Odyssey*. Suffice it to say, the works complement each other — down to the oddity of the last chapter of the *Odyssey* describing the funeral of Achilles, who was dead long before the story began.[21]

On the surface, the *Odyssey* is an adventure tale, charting the hero's long voyage home as he is confronted with one challenge after another, including witches, monsters, malevolent giants, angry gods, and natural calamities ranging from whirlpools to tempests. It is good fun for kids. It also casts the archetype of 'homecoming', which projects life as a long journey of trial and hardship that reaches its climax in returning to the place of easeful belonging and serenity. Home is the place where, as Odysseus himself puts it, 'death will drift upon me from seaward, mild as air'.[22]

The *Odyssey* is also a parable about how greed and folly double the suffering that is the lot of man. These are exactly the words that Zeus uses in line 50, near the start, proclaiming one of his divine laws. This story moves beyond the iron grip of Necessity. Humans play a role in what happens to them.

When the *Odyssey* is read as a tale of adventure and a blueprint for homecoming, positing a more relaxed fatalism than that projected in the *Iliad*, it lacks depth and bite. The poetry is bland compared with the *Iliad*. And the story describes a world overshadowed by Troy. Homer casts a storyteller, Demodokos, within his story, and what Demodokos sings about is Troy. Hades is populated mainly by ghosts from the Trojan War. Troy conjures up a memory of a greater time, one in which life was fuller and more real, when men were larger than life. It was a world of heroes, now lost. Without heroes, the human domain descends into anarchy — the state of Odysseus's island of Ithaka in his absence. Odysseus's wife, Penelope, suffers from twenty years of misery, set upon by unwelcome suitors; her son Telemachos is powerless to protect her. The bow of Odysseus, which he left at home during the war, becomes a metaphor for the new age of ordinary men. None of them, including Odysseus's own son, are strong enough to string it.

The *Odyssey* is pitched against the *Iliad*. It attempts to shift the culture, instating a new constellation of human values. Demodokos, the blind minstrel and muse who entertains the Phaiakian court in Book VIII, may be a projection of Homer himself, who, by repute, was blind. The story Demodokos sings is in praise of Odysseus as the greatest of men. Demodokos refers to a dispute between Odysseus and Achilles at Troy, when the two raged violently against each other during a feast. The implication is that the dispute was over who had the greatest claim to fame. Achilles is identified with *biē* (courage or force). He is the first among humans in this sphere.

Odysseus, by contrast, is the master tactician. As Jenny Strauss Clay puts it, he combines the leading characteristics of *mētis* (cunning intelligence, calculating quick-wittedness) with *dolos* (trickery and deceit). In this, he is the human counterpart of Athena, she being supreme among the gods with these traits.[23] He uses his quick wit and guile to conquer Troy through deploying the stratagem of the Trojan horse (an episode recounted by Demodokos). In the adventure with Polyphemos — the giant one-eyed Cyclops, son of Poseidon — Odysseus escapes by outsmarting dumb brutishness. He and his men are held prisoner in the Cyclops' cave. Odysseus tempts the man-eating giant with wine, getting him drunk, and then blinds him with a red-hot stake. The bellowing screams of pain that follow attract other Cyclops who live nearby. But, when they enquire from outside the closed cave as to what's happened, Polyphemos shouts, 'Nobody's tricked me.' So they depart without providing help. Odysseus has tricked the giant by having had the guile to tell him beforehand that his name is 'Nobody'.

Odysseus's own men are stupid and impulsive — they have no *mētis*. They disobey Odysseus, in spite of his severe warnings. When they become hungry, they kill the sacred cattle of the sun-god Helios. In their greed, they open Odysseus's bag and unwittingly free the winds. Their folly doubles the misfortune of their master.

Demodokos's second story in Book VIII is about craft and warrior excellence. In effect, it posits a contest between *mētis* and *biē*. The victory is awarded to Odyssean intelligence.[24] Further, Odysseus as the human ideal gains *nostos* (homecoming), by virtue of his cleverness. Achilles gains *kleos* (glory), but loses *nostos*. Odysseus gains both.

In her book *The Wrath of Athena*, Jenny Strauss Clay argues that Athena's anger at Odysseus orchestrates the plot of the second Homeric epic. Book III of the *Odyssey* indicates that the goddess is enraged with the Greeks during their sack of Troy, but no explanation is given as to the cause of her anger. In Book V, there is another reference to her punishing the Greeks as they sail home, but again no explanation is provided as to why. Athena usually protects and guides Odysseus, her single favourite now that Achilles is dead. But, for some reason, she is angry with him. As a consequence, it will take him ten years to voyage home.

Two possible causes surface as the story unfolds. Odysseus is too full of himself, and he lacks reverence. As he sails away from the defeated Polyphemos, he shouts out to the humiliated giant in bragging mockery. The Cyclops then hurls boulders after the departing ship, nearly sinking it. More seriously, Polyphemos's father, Poseidon, is outraged at Odysseus for blinding his son.

Poseidon is supported by Zeus in inflicting more hardships on the hero. Athena chooses not to intervene. At Phaiakia, Odysseus wants the court to hear how smart he is, by asking for a retelling of the story of the Trojan horse. This is boyish vanity.

Odysseus is too smart by half, and too full of his own trickery. In Book XIII there is a long and pivotal encounter with Athena herself, who appears disguised as a young man. It provides the key to the plot. Odysseus, blind to her identity, fabricates a long and elaborate fiction about who he is. She responds by giving him a caress and changing her look into that of a tall and beautiful woman. She chides him warmly:

> Whoever gets around you must be sharp
> and guileful as a snake; even a god
> might bow to you in ways of dissimulation.
> You! You chameleon!
> Bottomless bag of tricks! Here in your own country
> Would you not give your stratagems a rest
> Or stop spellbinding for an instant?[25]

Athena then reveals her identity, and reminds him she always shields him in times of trial. Odysseus remains wary. He distrusts her: he doubts both her claimed identity and what she has told him about him having arrived on his home soil. He protests that she has not protected him. Odysseus is guilty of a major transgression here. He does not trust the goddess, a lack of reverence which is compounded by his criticising her for having abandoned him. His lack of trust is on a par with his earlier attempt to deceive her about his identity; in effect, it is an attempt to outsmart her. And he offers no apology.

Jasper Griffin puts it that the most regular and typical of all expressions of Greek wisdom was, 'Remember that you are not a god.'[26] Even the Delphic 'Know thyself!' might be interpreted, 'Know that you are not a god!' or 'Know your place!' Achilles is commonly described by Homer as 'godlike'; Odysseus seems to covet the title, but with the transgressive twist that, at times, he behaves as if he thinks he is equal to the gods.

Athena is surprisingly forgiving about this impudence — by comparison, she once turned Arachne into a spider for having dared to challenge her skill in weaving. Odysseus is merely accused of detachment. Athena treats him like a mother treats a favourite son with whom she is not pleased. Bemused at his failure to grow up, she seems to overlook his assertion of himself as her equal — his presumption in taking her on in a battle of wits.

In part, Athena's tolerance follows from her strategic alliance with Odysseus, who is her human counterpart in the fight against barbarism, represented by Poseidon and Polyphemos. Just as she outsmarts Poseidon in every contest between them, Odysseus exemplifies the emergence of civilised humanity out of the primeval jungle, a humanity that by means of intelligence and will can forge the world to its own liking. Mind you, Odysseus naming himself 'nobody' to Poseidon's son might be read, sub-textually, as unconscious acknowledgement that he is a nonentity, as are all mortals: 'Remember that you are not a god!'

If the *Odyssey* is intended to promote *mētis* as the highest human value, replacing *biē*, it fails. The argument underestimates the Achilles of the *Iliad*, who is far more than just a mighty and courageous warrior. It also overlooks the degree to which the character of Odysseus is diminished. Jenny Strauss Clay indirectly admits the latter, in placing the *Odyssey* more in the tradition of comedy than tragedy, and identifying Odysseus with the post-heroic world of ordinary mortals.

Achilles is, in terms of exemplary character, the larger human being of the two. He may be less intellectually brilliant, but he gains tragic gravity. His words to Lykaon, 'Do you not see what a man I am, how huge, how splendid', are not uttered as a boast, but rather stand as a pained and detached reflection, steeped in doomed foreboding. Achilles comes of age through suffering.

Odysseus is a transitional figure. With one foot in the Trojan War, he belongs to the old order of heroes. Once he finally reaches home, after a twenty-year absence, it is this hero self that strings the bow and kills the suitors who have invaded his house, feasted on his provisions, and harassed his wife. But Odysseus has another self. It belongs to the new age of ordinary mortals. He is, in this new persona, the normal human male at its most capable — smart, practical, confident, independent, and crafty. He is an able leader, and a just and generous king, loved by his people.

Odysseus provokes the wrath of Athena because of *human* hubris, in contrast with the *hero* hubris of Achilles, which drove the warrior to excess on the field of battle. Odysseus is cocky and impudent; Achilles is berserkly out of control with grief and rage. Achilles corrects himself and, in his courtesy, becomes the more balanced man. Odysseus never changes; he does not achieve *sōphrosunē*. His trial is one of hardship, not suffering. He fails to undergo an initiation ordeal, through which his brash juvenile self is killed off, and out of which an adult in full maturity may emerge. Odysseus gains practical knowledge, not wisdom. Achilles is closer to the deeper spirit of their shared patron goddess, Athena. The onlooker is never moved to tears by the plight of Odysseus, never lowers the eyes in pity, and never gasps with awe in contemplating this man and his life. The contrast between the two protagonists is one of timeless and profound significance, as pertinent today as it has ever been.

Homer moves us from the orbit of the hero, characterised by might, glory, and gravity, to the orbit of the human, who is clever, cunning, and restless. The *mythos* chronology, however, is more complex. In spite of this historical shift, both types endure. They lead into an ever-present, eternal human drama: the contest between the hero and the best of men. The hero becomes shrouded in enigma, entering the dark world of Karyatid wisdom. The man gains home, a qualified glory, and paves the way for the Parthenon.

But the man, like his creation, the Parthenon, lacks depth. This leaves a residue of yearning in the human heart, a yearning for the hero. Just as our journey back in time, in quest of the *archē*, is driven by an obscure sense of primal belonging, the hero pipes a universal tune of a time and a place in which life was as it should be, and of a generation of men who truly lived. The tune conjures up the glistening image of a human presence, the shadow of a man 'huge and splendid' standing astride the plains of Troy — one whose poise of being might withstand anything, even the doubts and fears that hound mortality. Every nation locates its own particular *mythos* where heroes fought and died, whether it is England with its Agincourt, Trafalgar, and Waterloo; America with its Civil War; or Australia with its Gallipoli. The aura of Achilles magnetises every national culture in the West.

Alexander the Great spent his brief life trying to bring back the heroic world of Achilles. The last flower of Hellenic greatness, there was a wild and manic desperation to his adulthood as he flashed — a brilliant, unforgettable star — across the stage of world history.

Alexander was born in 356 BC, nine years before the death of Plato. He came into the world four centuries after Homer (which is the same time difference that separates us from Shakespeare). His father, King Philip II of Macedon, brought Aristotle to his court to tutor the boy when he was twelve. Aristotle, at the time in his early forties, spent four years forming the young Alexander's mind. At the age of twenty, Alexander became King of Macedon, following the assassination of his father. He would then rule for a mere thirteen years, dying of fever in Babylon in 323 BC. The empire he created included, in modern geographical terms, Greece, the Balkans north to the River Danube, Turkey, Syria, Lebanon, Israel, Egypt, Iraq, Iran, Afghanistan (and the various central Asian states to its north), Pakistan, and north-west India.

Alexander as a battle commander exemplified both *biē* and *mētis*. He led by example, fighting at the head of the Companion Cavalry, showing hair-raising and often near-fatal personal courage. The effect on the morale of his troops of his unstoppable volcanic fearlessness must have been infectious and immense — they loved their commander. The Duke of Wellington, a commander in Alexander's mould, displayed *biē* during the long day of the Battle of Waterloo, when he kept riding to the hottest areas of fighting; the danger he placed himself in is reflected in the twenty aides-de-camp who rode with him that day, most of whom were killed. One of his officers asserted, 'We would rather see his long nose in the fight than a reinforcement of ten thousand men.'[27]

Alexander destroyed the Persian Empire under Darius in a sequence of three victories — Granicus in 334, Issus in 333, and Gaugamela on 1 October 331. Military historian Victor Davis

Hanson judges Gaugamela 'the most brilliant victory in the history of East–West confrontation'.[28] On all occasions, the Macedonians were heavily outnumbered, which they expected and did not fear. At Gaugamela, Darius may have had 50,000 mounted troops, to Alexander's 8,000.[29] Alexander's victories provided a worthy sequel to the Athenian defeat of a vastly superior force of Persians at Marathon in 490 BC, an association that was important to him.

Alexander's strategy did not change. By the time of Gaugamela, Darius was well familiar with it, and the Persian king chose the field of battle on a plain to suit his own strengths — especially his chariots and elephants. He had amassed triple the number of Alexander's horse and infantry, yet he still lost. He could not match the spirit of the Macedonian troops; their level of training, experience, and organisation; nor the tactics of Alexander, which depended on coolness in the heat of battle, and timing. Alexander knew that, if he could maintain rank and break the enemy as a cohesive whole, he would always win.[30]

Alexander chose his old and very experienced general Parmenio to hold the left flank at Gaugamela, while he waited on the right. In the early fighting, Parmenio was nearly overwhelmed by Persian and Indian cavalry, who broke through in the centre, riding back to the Macedonian camp in the rear. Alexander continued to wait, in spite of the rapidly increasing danger of his left wing being annihilated. He had his troops drift slowly to the right, towards rough ground where Darius's scythed chariots would be incapacitated. This forced Darius's left wing ever further left to block the Macedonian movement. Meanwhile, as the battlefront stretched wider and wider, Alexander held back with his veteran cavalry, looking for a gap in the enemy's centre. Then he struck, with a mighty, concentrated single blow, forcing a hole in the Persian line. He charged straight through at Darius. The king panicked and fled.

Alexander had to call off his chase of the routed Persian king to return to aid Parmenio. By the end of the day, the Persian cavalry was almost completely wiped out. Five hundred Persians had fallen at Gaugamela for every Macedonian.

Alexander was more than a supreme warrior and commander. He was a founder of cities, and a cultivator of the arts. Wherever he conquered, he built cities, on the Greek model — a score of Alexandrias, and seventy cities altogether, came to dot the Middle Eastern and far-Eastern landscape. With the greatest of them all, Alexandria in Egypt, he himself laid down the markers for the city walls and the internal plan, designating the centre and the sites for the temples; some were dedicated to Egyptian gods, a sign of the conqueror's meta-Greek, universal perspective. The circuit of the walls was fifteen kilometres, an indication of Alexander's confidence about the future of his foundation. The city was to be self-governing, on the model of Athenian democracy, with public assemblies and magistrates. Alexander did not leave a garrison behind.[31] He had a vision for the civilised metropolis, one in which peoples of different cultures and with different beliefs could live and work together. Alexandria became exactly that, and remained so for over two millennia. It is fitting that the founder should have been buried there.

Alexander, under Aristotle's influence, developed an interest in zoology and botany. And he became an expert in medicine, concerning himself with his soldiers' wounds; he would minister to his friends' sicknesses. (Achilles, too, had been adept at healing.)[32] He was singularly open-minded, considering all men to be equal. He admired the Persians, and took up many of their ways and customs, including wearing their dress. His first wife, Roxana, was a Bactrian. He integrated Asians with Macedonians in his army. He did not enslave the peoples he conquered, contra the advice of Aristotle, who, like other Greeks, viewed them as 'barbarians'. Alexander respected their religion and customs, and left them to rule themselves as long as they pledged fealty to him. He trained administrators, and encouraged self-sustaining kingdoms. Alexander's own Macedonian officers and soldiers were bitterly resentful of his adoption of Eastern ways, and his treatment of barbarians as equal to his own people.

Alexander's passions were in tune with the classical Greek ideal. He loved extreme exercise, notably hunting. He was a runner of Olympic standard, but refused to enter the Games, 'unless I had kings to run against'. His pride would not countenance the fact that he might be awarded victory in a race because of his power, rather than on his own merits. Also, he held some disdain for professional athletics, which had become decadent in his time. He was a conversationalist and loved books, which he had shipped to him regularly in the depths of Asia. His favourite author was Homer; and, after him, the three tragedians, the poets, and Xenophon. He loved theatre and music. Artists would travel great distances to entertain him, and were received as guests not servants.[33] Finally, friendship was of supreme importance to Alexander, and he remained fiercely loyal to his friends. He was unhinged with grief when his companion and second-in-command, Hephaestion, died. Alexander fasted for three days in response.

Alexander set a standard in the West. He always slept with two things under his pillow: a dagger and a copy of the *Iliad* (his copy had been edited for him by Aristotle when he was a boy, and it was kept in an especially precious Persian casket). He claimed he learnt what he knew about the art of war from Homer. After crossing the Hellespont, he made a personal detour to visit the tomb of Achilles.

Alexander took Greek culture to the limits of the known world, and implanted it in the cities he founded. He gave birth to cosmopolitanism. He was the creator of the Hellenistic world, which still, three centuries later, continued to provide a universal pan-national language and culture across southern Europe and the Middle East. It framed the context, for instance, in which the four Lives of Jesus were written.

Some modern writers have vilified Alexander for burning down the magnificent royal palace at Persepolis, the centre of the Persian Empire.[34] But Alexander was the Hegemon, or leader, of the Greeks, as well as King of Macedon. He was responsible for the honour of the whole people. His campaign in the East was, in part, revenge for the Persian invasions of Greece in 490 BC, and especially 480 BC when the invaders burnt down the Acropolis in Athens. And he had to reward his long-suffering troops — which he did by licensing days of rioting, drunken debauchery.

Nevertheless, Alexander's record is deeply tarnished and paradoxical. His charm, cultivation, and military and political good sense were vulnerable to his own manic-depressive disposition. Plutarch puts it circumspectly:

> His society was delightful and his manner full of charm beyond that of any prince of his age. (Yet) he would sometimes become offensively arrogant and descend to the level of the common soldier, not only allowing himself to give way to boasting but also to be led on by his flatterers.[35]

He could be savage after victory. Once the two-month siege of Gaza in 331 BC had succeeded, he had 10,000 men killed. Thousands of women and children were sold into slavery. The local Persian commander, Batis, who was severely wounded, refused to speak to Alexander. Alexander, in a fury, imitated Achilles and ordered Batis's ankles to be pierced so he could be dragged around the city walls behind a chariot until he was dead.[36]

Alexander's manic-depressive disposition became more extreme and unbalanced in his last years. He became increasingly suspicious of the Macedonian officers who had provided the command backbone for his success, and had them steadily purged. At times, he displayed paranoia. Mind you (as Freud was later to point out), the paranoiac is not always wrong. There were indeed a string of plots to kill Alexander, one involving Parmenio's son, which led to Parmenio himself being killed on the king's orders. The paranoia included delusions of grandeur, a megalomania that demanded he be recognised as a god; this had been fuelled, Macbeth-like, by an oracle at Siwah in Egypt, who had declared him 'son of Zeus'. That his success and his glory as 'Lord of Asia' were of godly proportions was undeniable, but the Greek/Macedonian world was not inclined to bow down before mere humans. Alexander's self-immortalisation was a form of excess that even turned Aristotle, his mentor, away from him. He had transgressed that cautioning metaphysical law, central to Greek wisdom, 'Remember that you are not a god.'

Alexander plunged into more extreme bouts of drinking — two-day binges followed by two days to sleep them off. He withdrew in a sulk for three days in India when his officers rebelled, forcing him to turn back. When his bosom-companion Hephaestion died, he had Hephaestion's hapless doctor crucified. He had one of his own corps of 6,000 men decimated — one in ten of them, chosen at random, were killed.[37] (There are later parallels, here, in the life of Captain James Cook, a man who combined Alexandrian traits in his courage, excellence as a navigator, and vision as commander and captain. On his third and last voyage, Cook became erratic, his once peerless judgement deserting him.)

So Alexander's story ended up taking a quite different trajectory to that of his idol, Achilles. His vision and its glorious implementation fed an ever-greater sense of his own grandeur, which, in combination with his increasing psychological instability, turned his loyal officers and troops away from him. For Alexander, there was to be no equivalent to the grief of Achilles — detaching the hero from his glory, and serving to dignify him with a magisterial detachment and composure, and a higher generosity of spirit. Alexander's glory is complemented, not by a deepening in his own character, but by the vision he put into practice for universalising the best of Greek civilisation.

Why have I included Alexander in these reflections? It is he who brings Achilles out of the pages of *mythos*. He is the real-life Achilles. As such, he inspires a powerful and recurring lineage in the West. In the Anglo tradition, that lineage includes Shakespeare's Henry V, James Cook, the Duke of Wellington, and Winston Churchill.

Alexander gives birth to cosmopolitanism, shaped by the authority of Greek culture. The Greeks had already been colonisers — most notably in the form of the Athenian Empire, which included colonies that stretched from Sicily to the Black Sea, populated by expatriate Athenians. But those colonies had been parochial, undergirded by the Athenians' belief in their own superiority. Alexander extended and transformed this model into a multi-peopled, trans-ethnic Hellenism.

In effect, he integrated the ethos of Achilles with that of Odysseus. He took the Parthenon to the world. He launched the West's civilising tradition, centring on the democratic self-governing city, with legal institutions independent from either political or clerical power, and with everyday life conducted in a spirit of free, sceptical enquiry and religious tolerance. This is the metropolis that we in the West came to cherish, graced by beautiful temples, libraries, schools, academies, and sporting arenas.

HEAD OF HYGEIA, FROM TEMPLE OF
ATHENA ALEA, TEGEA (C 360 BC)

FIVE

ATHENA

Athena was referred to by fifth-century-BC Athenians as 'the god'. Modern scholars dispute whether she was named after the city, or the other way round (many other cities, including Troy, had her as a principal deity).[1] Either way, the identification of the city with its patron goddess was intimate and complete. In the modern West, we have no parallel to this; our metropolis is pervasively secular. Greek polytheism, or any equivalent, is long dead. The bare historical facts are that the Romans continued Greek religion, with their own adaptations, and then turned to monotheistic Christianity, which spread, and prevailed in the West for fifteen hundred years until recently.

So the ancient Greek stories about their gods should be culturally alien to us. Yet, in some perplexing way, this is not the case, or at least not entirely the case. For one thing, there has been the continuing influence of works in which the Greek gods play major roles, starting with the *Iliad*, but also including the *Odyssey*,

Agamemnon, *Oedipus*, *Antigone*, *Medea*, the *Bacchae*, and Plato's *Symposium*. I want to explore why. At issue, I think, is the need to give a plausible, concrete expression to the divine, in particular the need to personify it. A personalised god is closer to the human than the supreme, all-powerful God of the three monotheisms. Walter Otto writes of Greek religion as 'so natural that holiness seems to have no place in it.'[2]

We today might find a lot in common, in our view of the world, with fifth-century Athenians. The higher-class, better-educated citizens, already sceptical about much of the mythology attributed to their gods, and even about the literal existence of the gods, were lapsing into a detached philosophy of religion. You can see this in the works of the warrior and playwright Aeschylus, as when his chorus chimes, 'Zeus: whatever he may be.'[3] The philosophers Anaxagoras and Protagoras were, in modern terms, secular humanists, and both were friends of Perikles. Aristophanes, in his 423 BC satire on the new philosophy, *The Clouds*, identifies Socrates (if unfairly) with the relativist view: 'There never was Justice or Truth.' Two of the charges levelled against Socrates at his trial in 399 BC were that he mocked the city's gods, and that he gave profane, physical explanations for heavenly events.

I want to open this reflection on the goddess Athena — on who and what she was — by trying to imagine her place in Periklean Athens. Euripides is representative of the cultural elite: the one god he respects is Athena, identifying her with Athens, the two partly conflated in a spirit of sacred patriotism. Aristophanes subjects all the gods apart from Athena to mocking farce. Athena Parthenos is Athens, representing its highest ideal of itself. C. J. Herington claims that 'Athena's attributes, victorious prowess in war, intelligence, love of the arts, are precisely the attributes of the

Athenian people as Perikles describes them in the Funeral Speech.[34] But there is in this attitude some detachment: the identification is conscious, even self-conscious, rather than that of a visceral, unquestioning faith. The huge statue crafted by Pheidias, on display in the Parthenon, was not venerated as a religious icon. As far as we can tell from the sketchy historical records, she stood rather as a civic monument, with a role akin perhaps to that of the modern Statue of Liberty in New York. It is telling that she was decked ostentatiously in thick gold sheets, showing off the wealth of Athens.

The crude wooden statue of Athena Polias in the Erechtheion, with its archaic associations, was a more suitable object for the worship of Athenian traditionalists, and especially of the common people. It represented the type of communally binding religion approved of by the old Plato, in his final work, the *Laws* — his social conservatism pivoted on cult and ritual. Plato's attitude is typical of the intellectual philosophy or sociology of religion: it holds that communal religious practice is good for ordinary people, and for public morale, although the philosopher doesn't hold to any of its beliefs himself. Perikles may well have shared this attitude.

Whatever Plato's views about a society's political health, the fact was that Athena's city, Athens, in the great period from the victory over the Persians at Marathon in 490 to the death of Perikles in 429, was ruled over by a procession of extraordinarily gifted leaders: Themistokles, Kimon, Aristides, and Perikles in politics; and Miltiades, Themistokles, and others in battle. Once this age of great leaders came to an end, Athens steadily declined. It lost the thirty-year Peloponnesian War to the Spartans (who were far weaker economically). After the final defeat in 404 BC,

Athens never recovered its geo-political eminence, its wealth, or its self-confidence (with the exception of a brief golden period around 370 BC).

Thucydides wrote his *History of the Peloponnesian War* in order to try to understand the defeat of Athens. His work stands as the founding masterpiece of social and political analysis in the West. Thucydides drew the obvious lesson about leadership. The same lesson was to become basic to secular politics in the ages before the rise of modern parliamentary democracy: Shakespeare, for example, centred his history plays on linking the wellbeing of England to the strength and sagacity of its ruling king. For Thucydides, Athens' decline, which he observed as a citizen present at many of the key events, was entirely due to human fallibility — there were no supernatural causes.

The biography of Perikles is instructive. He was politically astute, moderate and balanced, and adept at diplomacy as he expanded the Athenian empire and held it together. He was an able military leader: when heading the naval suppression of the revolt of Samos in 440, he sent off the aristocrat and tragedian Sophocles as his successful ambassador to the islands of Chios and Lesbos, which had their own fleets, to ensure they didn't join the rebellion. Perikles' policy failed only in last two years of his life, partly due to him attributing too much rationality to the Spartans and the Corinthians, and not foreseeing that they would flare up in fear of increasing Athenian power; and partly due to a debilitating plague that struck the city and its navy in 429 BC.[5]

The Parthenon and the Erechtheion exist because of Perikles. His drive and influence, in combination with his aesthetic vision, rebuilt the Acropolis. As we have seen, he chose his gifted friend Pheidias to oversee the architecture, and to undertake the sculpture of Athena.

A new suppleness and vitality of life is displayed in the carvings of the Parthenon friezes; as such, they symbolise the Periklean spirit. In fact, Perikles the man and the leader is the human counterpart in public life to the Parthenon, exemplifying its ethos.

Perikles was a paragon of *sōphrosunē*. He did not party at night; on occasion, when he joined a celebration, he would leave when the drinking started. He did not share the misogynist tendencies of many of his contemporaries, preferring to spend evenings with his de-facto wife, the ex-courtesan Aspasia. Otherwise, his evenings were spent in discussion with his two philosopher friends Anaxagoras and Protagoras. He built the Odeion for indoor music and poetry, contributing to the high prestige in which poets, musicians, and men of letters were held.

Perikles' famous Funeral Oration, delivered to honour those first to die in the Peloponnesian War, reflected on the character of Athens, of its people and their political constitution. Its principles and its sentiments have not dated. He described Athenian virtue, in effect, as a synthesis of Achilles and Odysseus:

> We Athenians, in our own persons, take our decisions on policy or submit them to proper discussions: for we do not think there is an incompatibility between words and deeds; the worst thing is to rush into action before the consequences have been properly debated. And this is another point where we differ from other people. We are capable at the same time of taking risks and estimating them beforehand. Others are brave out of ignorance; and, when they stop to think, they begin to fear. But the man who can most truly be accounted brave is he who best knows the meaning of what is sweet in life and of what is terrible, and then goes out undeterred to meet what is to come.[6]

Already, one-hundred-and-fifty years earlier, this Athenian practical wisdom had been on display. The great law-giver, Solon, replied to Croesus of Lydia, the richest man in the world, who had asked him who was the happiest of mortals:

> Tellus of Athens {an unknown}. Tellus' polis was prosperous, and he was the father of noble sons, and he saw children born to all of them, and they all grew up. And after a life spent in what among our people passes for comfort, he dies most gloriously. In a battle between the Athenians and their neighbours near Eleusis, he came to the aid of his fellow-citizens, turned the enemy to rout, and died most nobly. The Athenians game him a public burial on the spot where he fell {only the men who died at Marathon received the same extraordinary honour} and honoured him greatly.[7]

What I have been outlining seems to have been a very worldly culture. It was shrewdly practical, utilising disciplined and trained intelligence; thoughtful and sceptical, enjoying power, wealth, and glory; and patriotic, celebrating its achievements with grand public buildings, aesthetic and sporting feats, and extravagant festivals.

But fifth-century Athenians, whatever the levels of critical scepticism in the upper class, believed in the *divine*. Aeschylus brooded for the entire stretch of his masterpiece, *Agamemnon*, in quest of the higher meaning that might give sense to dark and squalid events. Sophocles, in the quintessential Greek tragedy *Oedipus the King*, proclaims the central truth about the human condition to be the implacability of fate. Socrates always deferred to his *daimon*; and he attributed all he knew about love, in Plato's *Symposium*, to what he had been told by a prophetess, Diotima.

Athens held its major festival, the Panathenaia, every four years.

It was dedicated to Athena: its processions, its athletics, and its feasts were all held in celebration of the goddess. Under Perikles, the city gave magnificent prizes to the winners. The festival opened with a procession from the Pompeion delivering a newly woven *peplos* (or cloak) to dress the wooden statue of Athena Polias. (The procession is celebrated in one of the friezes on the Parthenon.) In the evening, a torch race brought fire to the altar, where sacrifices were made, followed by all-night celebrations, dancing, and musical competitions. The next day, there were gymnastic events; foot races; the pentathlon (jump, foot race, discus, javelin, and wrestling); races in armour; boxing and wrestling; and horse events, including racing, four-horse chariot racing, and javelin throwing from horseback.[8] On the fifth day, there were team events, including mock battles. This is 'athletic religion', a hymn of praise to the city and its presiding goddess. The latter half of the fifth century saw an extraordinary profusion of images of Athena displayed throughout the city.[9]

Perikles used Athens' riches to build temples. Was this out of a canny sense of the role of civil religion in building patriotic identity and enthusiasm, or was there more to it? He asserted in his Funeral Oration that Athens had no need of a Homer — implying that it could, through its own creations and acts, display and celebrate its greatness.

The Parthenon sculptures represent the gods, with pride of place given to Athena. What is new in them, compared with what has come before in Greece, is not that the gods are removed or even diminished; it is that in some friezes, Athenians are raised in status so as to interact almost as equals with the gods.

This is a culture, then, in which Homer and Thucydides sit side by side, on twin thrones. The *Iliad* is the sacred text, the Bible that enshrines the ideal of the hero, and his right relationship to *sōphrosunē*, to the gods, and to fated tragedy. Thucydides, on the other side, exemplifies practical, secular thinking about politics, diplomacy, war, human character, and his own society's strengths and weaknesses. Perikles was of the Thucydides temper in his leadership and in his choice of philosopher friends with whom to discuss life and its meaning. At the same time, his Oration is rich in Homeric cadences, and his Parthenon stands as a transcendent form, fusing human and divine, existing both in the world and beyond it.

Now let me focus on the goddess herself. The most telling of Athena's interventions in the *Iliad* occurs at the start of Book 18. When Achilles is told of the death of Patroklos, a 'black cloud of sorrow' closes over him as he collapses into the dust. He is suicidal with grief. But the agony is slowly assuaged by anger, driving him to take revenge on Hektor. Hektor has not only killed Patroklos, but left his body naked, having stripped it of Achilles' own armour, which had been given to his father, Peleus, by the gods. Hektor is, at this moment, triumphing in battle, wearing the armour of Achilles on his shoulders, 'glorying in it'. Achilles will delay his own death by the one thing he still desires: to avenge Patroklos. He knows that it is decreed that soon after the death of Hektor, he too must die; by killing the Trojan hero, he brings on his own end.

Meanwhile, the fighting continues close by, as the Trojans surge towards the Greek ships. Achilles' anger rises, 'smoking in his breast', yet 'sweet like honey', as he himself describes it. The goddess Hera sends him the message that the Trojans are about to seize the body of Patroklos, which Hektor will drag off to Troy, before hacking off the head to exhibit on a stake, feeding the rest of the body to the dogs. Achilles protests to the messenger that he has no armour, and will be without any until the next morning, when a new suit will be brought to him by his mother — one made especially for him by the blacksmith god, Hephaestos. The messenger simply urges, 'Go to the ditch, and show yourself as you are to the Trojans.'

At this point, Athena intervenes:

> Achilleus, the beloved of Zeus, rose up, and Athene
> swept about his powerful shoulders the fluttering aegis;
> and she, the divine among goddesses, about his head circled
> a golden cloud, and kindled from it a flame far-shining
> As when a flare goes up into the high air from a city
> from an island far away, with enemies fighting about it
> who all day long are in the hateful division of Ares
> fighting from their own city, but as the sun goes down signal
> fires blaze out one after another, so that the glare goes
> pulsing high for men of the neighbouring islands to see it,
> in case they might come over in ships to beat off the enemy;
> so from the head of Achilleus the blaze shot into the bright air.
> He went from the wall and stood by the ditch, nor mixed with
>   the other
> Achaians, since he followed the close command of his mother.
> There he stood, and shouted, and from her palace Pallas Athene
> gave cry, and drove an endless terror upon the Trojans.
>
> As loud as comes the voice that is screamed out by the trumpet
> by murderous attackers who beleaguer a city
> so then high and clear went up the voice of Aiakides.

> But the Trojans, when they heard the brazen voice of Aiakides,
> the heart was shaken in all, and the very floating-maned horses
> turned their chariots about, since their hearts saw the coming
> afflictions.
> The charioteers were dumbfounded as they saw the unwearied
> dangerous
> fire that played above the head of great-hearted Peleion
> blazing, and kindled by the goddess grey-eyed Athene.
> Three times across the ditch brilliant Achilleus gave his great cry,
> and three times the Trojans and their renowned companions were
> routed.

This scene is pivotal in the *Iliad*, serving as one of the climaxes of narrative intensity that anchor the story. And what is the imagery that lodges indelibly in the mind of the reader, or listener? It is the golden aura shining from Achilles' head, like a flaming beacon. This aura is complemented by the three blood-curdling shouts, as he stands alone and unarmed by the ditch in front of the walls protecting the Greek encampment, bellowing his rage and his grief out across the battling armies. The first great shout is laced with Athena's own cry; it is amplified by the tones of her sacred rage. Her special, even singular, interest in this moment is indicated by her active participation, which is unusual — her presence is normally enough.

The goddess is the source of the hero's brilliance and his might. She is his radiance, what makes him more than ordinary, more than mortal. He is not alone on the field of battle — if he were, he would fail. The signal is, to one and all who follow Achilles in the West: if you stand completely on your own, without the infusion of some supernatural presence, you will fail. You will fail even if you have been endowed with godlike might, talent, and beauty.

I have opened with the *Iliad* because Homer's vision creates the archetype for all that will follow. Walter Otto puts it thus:

> The Greek genius must have received the figures of its religion and its worship in pre-Homeric times, for in Homer they are fixed, and ... they remained basically what they were for Homer. To find one's world is tantamount — whether for a people or for an individual — to finding one's self, to attaining realization of one's own character. The period whose conception of the world we learn from Homer is therefore the period of genius in Hellenism.[10]

Already, in the *Iliad*, Athena is the pre-eminent divinity. The formal hierarchy positions her as second to her father, Zeus, and even then that is a position she shares with other leading gods and goddesses. In terms of the significance of roles in the Homeric drama, three gods stand out: Zeus, Athena, and Apollo. Yet it is Athena and Hera, championing the Greeks, who get their way as to the course of the Trojan War. While Zeus nominally keeps order and decides events, the powerful women play him, realising their own ends. Otherwise, Hera has a limited role, and she is caricatured in the wider mythology as a spiteful, jealous wife. Apollo, backing the Trojans, is also powerful, and independent — it is he who will engineer the death of Achilles.

The precedence of Athena is given vast mythic projection in the story of her birth. Her mother was Metis, she of wise counsel. Zeus devoured the pregnant Metis, out of fear of what she might give birth to; according to one story, the progeny would be more powerful than lightning, the king-god's own most potent weapon.

Hephaestos assists at the birth by using a double-edged axe to crack Zeus's skull open. Athena then sprang out from the cleft in the sacred head of the father, fully clad in gold armour, brandishing a javelin, and screaming forth an earth-shaking battlecry.[11] The golden radiance that shines from the head of Achilles as he stands beside the field of battle on the plains of Troy, a radiance cast by Athena, thus repeats her own birth, with fire flaming forth from the head.

The symbolism is wild, extraordinary, and evocative. The father's head is split open by an axe wielded by one of his sons; the daughter leaps out fully developed, clad in golden armour, taking on the world with a victorious, blood-curdling warcry. The father, the king-god known for his wise counsel, looks on, and is mightily pleased, in spite of nursing a splitting headache.

What is important is sited in the head. The Greek *genesis* holds that, in the beginning, God created Athena out of his own mind. Then followed the time of the heroes — humans who were more than human, godlike, who set the terms in which those who followed should try to live their lives. The heroes were protected by the goddess.

The father's head is like a seedpod, splitting open to release new life, which is both warlike and wisely intelligent. The English word *conception* captures the dichotomy: the new conception is not biological, emerging from the mother's womb, but mental. However, it is not born 'out of mind', abstractly and intellectually (as in a philosophy seminar), but with dynamic physicality. In a blaze of golden light exploding from the splintered head, a radiant goddess emerges with a great shout — all presaging a new human order.

She would commonly be known as Pallas Athena, with *pallas* meaning 'strong virgin'. She was the warlike virgin. Likely, this was necessary for her to stand as an equal to men, without relying on traditional female powers. She was different from Hera, who used the magic of female deception to seduce her husband; or Aphrodite, who used her beauty to excite *eros*, and thereby gain power over men, and who was attracted to brute masculinity, personified by the war-god Ares. Athena tames men, in their archaic phallic mode: she outsmarts Poseidon, she resists Hephaestos, and, in the thick of battle in Book 21 of the *Iliad*, she flattens Ares. Yet she took no pleasure in war — unlike Ares — preferring to settle disputes and to provide the context for fruitful human community. In times of peace she did not bear arms, and even statues of her fully armed often show her as composed and nonchalant.[12] The new order she represents balances traditional male and female polarities, integrating them.

Athena's feminine side is reflected in the olive. The tree itself is austere, ruggedly resistant to heat and drought, virtually unkillable. Yet the oil nurtured within its fruit is mild, silky, and singularly beneficial to human health. Olive oil is useful, and for many purposes — from cooking, to anointing, to fuelling lamps. The olive grove is itself calm, with a self-contained serenity that is especially conducive to twilight reflections. Jesus submerged himself in his own last meditations, alone at night, in an olive grove in Jerusalem.

Athena's femininity is equally reflected in the Erechtheion. This, the other pole, is the site of the darker female mysteries, of occult powers, and of secret women's business. The knowing eyes of the Karyatids threaten to turn to stone any mortal who approaches them unwittingly.

From the fifth century, her characteristic look was established: a serene but aloof beauty, deep-set eyes, a high-bridge nose carrying up into the forehead, a narrow mouth with full lips, and a long neck. Yet Athena's femininity is heavily qualified. The virgin warrior is, in part, a mannish figure. There is not a hint of erotic sensuality nor, even, of soft feminine warmth. Her sex is unnatural, in that she is a male creation, not born of a woman. She reflects Athenian misogyny, or, perhaps more accurately put, the typical Athenian male's ambivalence towards female potency — both fearing it and needing its succour. Nevertheless, Athena does not project her own chaste disgust of the sexual onto humans: she is happy to bathe both Odysseus and his wife, Penelope, in golden beauty when they first meet after a twenty-year separation, to rekindle their desire for each other.

The Homeric projection of Athena as the protector of heroes changes in fifth-century Athens to that of the protector of the city.[13] She becomes domesticated, with her imagined role shifting from the heroic (inspiring heroes) to the homely (helping in ordinary life). Her favourite crafts, of which she is the patron, are metalwork and, for women, spinning and weaving.[14] The *peplos* was a rectangular woollen cloth decorated with scenes of the battles between giants and the gods led by Zeus and Athena. The special religious status accorded to it was a tribute to women, who would have spent most of their time, apart from preparing food, in spinning and weaving. Select women wove the *peplos* for an annual ceremony in Athens, except for the year of the Panathenaia. They would dress the cult statue in it.[15] In this period, Athena the virgin warrior is transformed into the mother of Athens. She is imagined as the surrogate mother of Erechthonius, the first king of Athens, whom she nurtured from infancy, and later protected.

This domestic Athena faded in later Western consciousness. I suspect this is due to the pre-eminent role of Homer in giving birth to Greek culture as we have inherited it. It is Homer's conception that drew the cultural blueprint that would shape the West. The city of Athens' projection of Athena as local, domestic, and motherly was parochial, and for that reason would soon lapse.

Otto designates Athena as the 'goddess of nearness'.[16] The heroes, Achilles and Odysseus, experience her as close by in times of trial. Odysseus prays to her, 'you who ever stand beside me in all hard tasks.'[17] She advises, she encourages, and she inspires. Further, there is an Orphic verse stressing Athena's dependency on her hands. With her crafts, she is also nearby in everyday life.[18]

Both the Homeric warrior and the Olympic athlete, as described by the poets, experience a god breathing through them, or moving beside them, when they triumph. Athena is not alone in playing this role, but she is the exemplar. Pindar, in his fifth *Isthmian Ode*, celebrates a generalised 'divine one':

> Because of you men prize gold in its great strength
> Beyond all other possessions;
> And in rivalry
> Ships on the sea and horses in chariots
> Are marvelled at, lady, because of your glory,
> As they contend in fast-eddying races.[19]

The German poet Hölderlin reflected on the nature of the Greek gods, and on what we have lost from their absence. He opens his poem, *Patmos*:

> Nah ist
> Und schwer zu fassen der Gott.
>
> (Near is
> And hard to grasp the god.)

The divine presence is close by, but tantalisingly elusive — very difficult to engage.

This is not the Athena of either of the statues on the Acropolis: the massive civic monument, Athena Parthenos, or the archaic wooden fetish, Athena Polias. It is Homer's Athena. The heroes battling before Troy were more than mere, ordinary mortals, in great part because they were closer to the gods. The favoured ones could feel the divinity breathing through them, feeding a greater vitality into their limbs; broadening their shoulders and filling out their chests; bathing their heads in golden light; adding resonance to their voices; clarifying their vision; or checking foolish impulses and unwise steps. Even Socrates listened to his *daimon*.

This is not a mystical religion. The individual does not withdraw in contemplation, attempting to commune with the beyond. The divine is very much in the world — immanent in human action. This religion draws upon human powers, rather than conjuring up miracles. Nor does it invite prayer, or any type of human pleading to change its will. When a god suddenly emerges close by, he or she comes not because the hero has invoked it, or longed for it, but as a blessing, or a gift, and entirely on its own terms. Likewise, the gods are not moral overseers — with the exception that they do frown on some excesses, in humans but not in themselves.

Athena is, first and foremost, a supernatural being. She dwells in a world beyond human comprehension. Yet she is not interested in the transcendental or the ethereal. Her concern is for the practical and the functional, for what works successfully on the human plane. That concern is principally focused on the individuals whom she favours. In all of this, she presides over a this-worldly individualism — one that will come to characterise the Western psyche, and underpin the greatness of its achievements.

Athena may have been born from her father's head, but she is best known by her eyes. *Glaukōpis*, coined by Homer, is one of a few recurring adjectives used to describe her. She herself nominates 'grey-eyed' as the term of endearment used by her father Zeus, the most intimate for his favourite daughter: 'There will come a day when he will again call me his dear *glaukōpis*.'[20] The adjective translates variously as 'gleaming-eyed', 'grey-eyed', and 'owl-eyed'. *Glaukōpis* in its original Homeric usage may have meant 'she of the gleaming eyes'.[21] 'Grey-eyed' or 'grey-blue-eyed' is also a literal translation, and has some association with the colour of the olive leaf, with its bluish-grey hue. 'Owl-eyed' has special Athenian resonance, in that the *glaux* was a little local owl, so-called because of its 'glaring' eyes. The owl, regarded as the wisest of birds, became the emblem of Athens, linked with Athena (although there is some contradiction between 'glaring' and 'knowing').

The owl, the bird known for seeing at night, evokes insight into dark knowledge. The large, round eyes look on with cool detachment, seeing everything. The owl is an unnerving presence, as if its reason for existing is to play the role of an eternal witness, a witness with forbidding judgement. There is special affinity here with the Karyatids. So the Greek genesis inaugurates a symbolic shift, from the head of the father to the night eyes of the daughter! The owl is a queer, strange-looking bird, appearing at night to be all head and eyes, without a body. It is as if thinking and seeing have taken over the whole corpus.

Yet those eyes are, in their beginning, gleaming eyes. They glitter with determination, alight with intensity of attention. We might imagine them as *shining* eyes. They counter the detached judgement of owl wisdom. Some sculpted heads of Athena that have survived conjure up an intensely powerful human presence.[22]

Humans with a gleam in their eyes provide the cue to a dynamic, vital engagement, as if preying on life, taking it in a firm grip, and squeezing it to extract all its worth. She is both nearby and full-on.

In this chapter, so far, I have rehearsed the basic facts about the classical Greek Athena. The defining contours of her image were drawn by Homer, and the main elaborations occurred in fifth-century Athens. Yet these surface facts no more than gesture towards whom or what she was.

To a sceptical modern mind, the most plausible reading is that 'Athena' was a human projection of a cluster of ideal qualities and strengths, and a means for giving shape to and celebrating sublime human moments, feelings of inspiration, and feats of extraordinary achievement.

Walter Otto glorifies such a view of the Greek gods. He does so most persuasively in the case of the goddess of love and beauty, Aphrodite. He puts it that:

> From her comes not so much the ecstasy of desire as the charm which kindles and propels it. She is the enchantment that radiates from things and beings and enraptures the senses with its smile. Not only men and beasts but plants, inanimate images and appearances, even thoughts and words, derive their winning, moving, overwhelming sweetness from her. And so her enchantment brings into being a world where loveliness moves toward delight, and all that is separated desires blissful fusion into oneness. In it all possibilities and desires are included, from dark animal impulse to yearning for the stars.[23]

Otto does catch here, maybe, the flavour of the goddess of divine *eros*, as she was revered in ritual and homage. He excludes from his picture the capricious side of Aphrodite. She was equally known for her narcissism, her fickleness, and her coquettishness — traits highlighted in Renaissance paintings of her. My hunch is that, to the modern imagination, attributing the power of *eros* to a supernatural entity is superfluous and faintly ridiculous. Otto doesn't attempt a similar personification of Athena.

Let me approach Athena from a different direction. In trying to grasp something beyond our normal ken, we have little more than our own experience to guide us. Experience feeds, firstly, our intuitions and intimations. Experience provides, secondly, the one standard for making us honest with ourselves — responding to the taunt of Kierkegaard, who questioned which philosophers have ever managed to think in the categories in which they actually lived. And, thirdly, experience serves as a tuning fork, sounding out how truly a story, a theme, or an image rings.[24] Intuition, harnessed to experience, is the one instrument we have for detecting the false note.

The metaphysical quest of our classical Greek forebears rings truly when tested by the tuning fork of modern experience. The Greeks were wise about the things beyond, and in ways that may help pick up and give shape to our own glimmerings. My working hypothesis is that their leading goddess must have dwelt among the important truths. Plato called her 'the mind of god'.

But to start once again at the beginning, our beginning, which is here and now: what can we glean from our own metaphysical experience?

There are two domains in which modern secular individuals may sense that they are subject to some higher force, or forces. There are two domains in which the gods may seem to be near. Taking my opening cue in this book from the Acropolis in Athens, I have signified these domains by using the terms 'Shining', with a capital 's', and Karyatid 'dark saying'.

Shining is life. It is life when it is rich, iridescent, and lifted above the normal material plane — when it is great to be alive, when we walk with a light step, and when we smile with radiance. Our eyes gleam; our skin glows. Breathing an intoxicating air, it is as if some superior presence and energy has possessed us — we are no longer our tiresome, bungling, lacklustre, ordinary selves.

Modern romance is written about, filmed, and articulated in transcendental imagery: 'Heaven is in your arms' and 'You're my dream angel.' Perhaps less ephemeral is the serious and untarnished language of the 'soul-mate', the single person chosen by destiny, or whatever, as the one true companion for life, and even longer.

The heroes of the modern action-film are projected as if they are descendents of 'godlike Achilles', moving with superhuman poise, carrying out superhuman feats of courage and might, indomitable in the face of normal human opposition. *Crouching Tiger; Hidden Dragon* (2000), a brilliant Chinese midrash of the American Western, even bestowed on its warriors the power to fly, and to duel in mid-air. In more modest ways, the central characters in many television series — police and medical dramas stand out — approach their work with religious-like devotion, as if much more is at stake in their job than its rational, practical ends. The pervasive modern ideal of work as a vocation taps into the same metaphysical source: this is the central life-task, what the person was meant to do, the 'calling' that brings meaning to the whole.

Modern sport holds the best players to be 'stars', even gods; leading venues are revered as sanctuaries where fans make pilgrimages to witness superhuman feats on the 'sacred turf'. Opening ceremonies at Olympic Games deliberately conjure up an opulent fantasia of mythic creatures, gods, spirits, and devils, before the sacred flame is lit, all to bathe the 'athletic religion' that is to follow in a magical, transcendental aura.

In short, modern Western life is rich with such secular renditions of divine Shining. As my brief catalogue here indicates, those renditions come in many and diverse forms.

Opposite the Shining, and in stark, dark contrast to it, are the Karyatid stone maidens. What they project is foreboding and dread. Somewhere in their depths lurks the Medusa stare. Necessity is cold. Fate is hard, pitiless, and implacable. The Karyatids look through the eyes of death.

Dark knowing may be triggered, today, by a heightened clarity of feeling and perception, induced by threat or momentous change. Life has dramatically shifted gear, switching out of ordinary time into a more epic, almost timeless, pace of events. A sense of script is awakened, that 'it was meant to be', or the opposite, in recoil, 'I'm sure that wasn't meant to be.' *I am on a path which is set. A sixth sense tells me that this is destined.* People have premonitions. They feel drawn by more than physical attraction, material ambition, or the opportunity for fame and fulfilment. Within, it is as if a drive, like an unconscious form of willpower, responds to a haunting, mysterious tune playing to them from beyond. That drive takes over. Or there is the opposite constellation of emotions, dominated by a feeling of being trapped in things that are bound to be, leading to a resigned shrug of the shoulders and a weary fatalism.

In these singular and momentous times, a guide may appear, if we are fortunate, to help us steer through a difficult life-passage. It may seem like an inner voice, or a sudden confidence about what to do when faced with a sequence of hard choices — choices that would normally paralyse us with strong feelings of apprehension about the possible consequences of making wrong decisions, fearing the 'What ifs?' Choices which elude rational decision are now, paradoxically, clear and easy to make. Such firmness of purpose through difficulty and challenge can be quietly exhilarating.

In these times, too, we may gain a sense of detachment, bringing us composure and equanimity in circumstances in which we would normally be rattled and panicky. In place of teeming thoughts and a rush of stratagems, we have gained a type of wisdom that will help us bear up to what has to be. We have joined Kassandra in her pronouncement: 'I will take my fate!' Most reassuring is our sense that there has been a transformation of consciousness: we have entered a larger, expanded metaphysical domain, in which we are a part of some grander, universal Oneness, subject to laws beyond our ken.

Today, we struggle to express what we experience in such extraordinary moments or times. We struggle, as I have here, to give shape to the most important things. We have largely lost our old metaphysical languages, and failed to find new, plausible ones. Classical Greek culture moved through precisely this territory with virtuosity and a sureness of instinct. Here was the core of its genius. That genius was led by Homer, and lay in the *mythos* it created. The Greeks wove the human through the divine, and vice versa. I suspect that here is the key to why the West has continued to respond to this tune, as to none other.

Why did the ancient Greeks need Athena? The Athenians chose her to embody their aspirations for themselves, as an ideal reflection of their virtues and capacities; they chose her to check their excesses and counter their weaknesses; and they chose her to garland their triumphs. Homer, who was closer to the domain in which the gods dwell than the fifth-century Athenians, and certainly closer than we are, evoked a more metaphysically charged world. The distance between hero and god was narrow, and relations between the two were unselfconscious and natural. A spectral quality colours the events that happen on the plains of Troy.

But maybe there is more to it. Maybe Athena forced herself on the Greeks. The individual 'I', now as always — the presence that is suddenly there once the person has entered the room — is a composite. It is more than physical contours and masses, gestures, smells, and sounds; character traits; or even a sum of past actions. There is a phantasmal core. Each living human is composed of a legion of personae, a multiple of shadowy selves, which move in and out of focus, and do so according to some logic that is impenetrable to the mortal mind. Some of these personae are supernatural, and as such they are 'hard to grasp'.[25]

Achilles knows that he is not alone as he stands unarmed beside the ditch, his head suddenly and miraculously shining with a golden flame. Is it a part of his deeper self that has suddenly flared forth, resplendent; or has he been joined by the invisible goddess, finding himself bathed in her light? Or both? Likely he is not sure, just as the Trojans are not sure. We, too, cannot be sure.

Standing on the Acropolis in Athens, it is difficult, even today, to believe that such a pure, transcendent form as the Parthenon was not guided, in its construction, by the hand of a divinity. As one approaches the grim, foreboding faces of the Karyatids, it is difficult to doubt that the dark temple behind and beneath them houses *daimonic* forces, ones that mere mortals toy with at their peril. In Apollo's sanctuary in Delphi, the air and the mood tell of some extraordinary, higher realm.

Homer sets the scene for flashes of divine intervention by charging nature with a wild, evocative quality of enchantment. The forces of the earth and the skies, the rivers and the seas, the climate, and the animals and the birds, breathe through Homer with an intimacy, directness, and intensity as if the poet and they were lovers. These are profane powers which, at the same time, carry a daimonic vitality that bathes the heroes who move through them with a supernatural aura. Heroes, when they move and act with excellence, are conjoined with nature, as with Diomedes, who goes 'storming up the plain like a winter-swollen river in spate'.

The gods are, viewed from one perspective, supernatural equivalents of natural forces, like metamorphosed extensions or projections. It is not a large imaginative leap from the winter-swollen river in spate, with its source in mighty nature, to the far-shining golden flame cast by Athena.

The Athena persona balances Shining and dark saying. The presiding goddess contains within herself the two cultural orders proposed in this book. There is the Shining of the Parthenon, of the Delphi Charioteer, and of Achilles bathed in her golden light, dazzling on the field of battle, sublime in the courtliness with which he conducts funeral games. She equally embodies the Karyatid counter-pole: the song of Kassandra, the steely eyes of the Medusa that Oedipus gradually makes out through the mists of his fate, and the wisdom of Achilles crushed by suffering. In this view of culture and life, Athena is all.

Yet she is not all, when it comes to summing up the totality of Greek culture. There was, in addition, Necessity (*anagkē*), colouring the background. The principal role of Necessity was that of scripting destiny for mortals, which she did through her three daughters, the Fates. The Greeks were so intimidated by Necessity that she

CHARIOTEER, DETAIL

was not personified — no representations of her face or even her silhouette appear in Greek art. She is a sort of super-divine, shadow force. She never appears, only being known to humans indirectly, through the events — usually dire — in which she ensnares them. Apollo comments that his powers are negligible next to those of Necessity.[26] Even he could not save his protégé, Hektor, once the scales of fate had tipped against him.

Because of Necessity, there had to be Apollo, her personified interpreter. He was distant and aloof, in contrast with his half-sister, whom mortals find nearby in times of duress. Apollo presides over the Oracle who foretells judgement, the binding judgement of Necessity. He leads the Muses who craft the truths that derive from her authority. He provides music to soothe the pain. And, as the sun god, he compensates for the darkness she projects, for Necessity crushes all hope.

Delphi is Apollo's domain. Athena's presence there is subordinate. That Delphi has been as important in these reflections as the Acropolis in Athens signals the independence of the sun god.

We humans wrestle with the eternal enigma. In the Olympic Opening Ceremonies, we lose ourselves today, if we are unselfconscious enough, in a fantastic dream-world of mythic creatures. Likewise, at Delphi, we may find ourselves captivated, taken beyond our familiar everyday selves, in a sanctuary cast somewhere in-between, mediating earth and heaven. Nearby are the gleaming eyes, intently watching, but hard to grasp. They cannot amend what is fated, but they can help illuminate the journey, invigorate the voyager, and bring to the passage some grace.

Wrath sing, goddess ... (*Mēnin aeide, thea ...*). So it begins, the story, its first three words in Greek signalling the subject, the mode, and the source. The story is not told by a mere mortal, Homer. If it were, it would be ephemeral, of passing interest, limited to one time and place. Homer knows that a divinity speaks through him — a muse. He is the servant, with his role that of poet-mouthpiece. The Greeks imagined the muses as semi-divine personifications of inspiration. And artists today follow Homer in continuing to refer to their 'muse'. But the father of Western narrative went further. It is as if the muse was not enough on her own, so he heard the voice of the goddess, too. At the opening of the *Odyssey*, Homer is explicit:

> From some point
> here, goddess, daughter of Zeus, speak, and begin our story.[27]

The source of the story is Athena, or so it seems, to the poet as to us. Plato, in designating Athena as the 'mind of god', may have been reflecting on this role. What we, the listeners, are about to hear is divine truth, crafted by the immortal hand, bestowing on it timeless authority. It will preside over every time and place, as if set in stone, the greatest of the ancient Greek monuments. It will be true *everywhen* — coming from a time before, in the beginning, and carrying us, whenever we tune in to it, outside normal time, and into the beyond.[28]

Here is the prototype of *mythos*. The surface story is particular, but what it articulates is universal — just as, in a simulated parallel, every listener has his or her own particular story, traversing their own Trojan plains. However, once they become enthralled by the goddess's song, captured by it, the sub-text will take them over, translating them into its own categories and motifs. Its radiance should then reflect back on their particular story, like a flame far-shining, intensifying and clarifying it, seizing hold of it and metamorphosing it into something larger and grander — even epic. Athena, incarnate in her song, is near.

An obscure but vital dimension of *mythos* is the presence of the supernatural. Mark, in his Life of Jesus, will work this in an intriguing fashion: from having his central character dance across the Sea of Galilee in the middle of the night to ending his tale with an enigmatic young man dressed in white sitting inside an empty tomb, telling the reader not to be alarmed. Of course, in our ordinary and everyday particular stories, we do not walk on water; but once possessed by the *mythos*, what is not possible? The young man in white, too, is not as he seems. For example, he may be the narrator. And, John, in retelling this episode, turns him into two angels dressed in white — a pair of divine narrators. Mark and John follow in Homer's steps, making their own adaptations.

Phantasmal things happen within the story, and the story itself is woven from sacred thread. When Athena intervenes personally in Homeric action, more is going on than it seems. She is a kind of midwife for some of the key events, in a story that she herself composes. In the scene in which her shout conjoins with that of Achilles, the presence is explicit. But the shout also serves as a cue to her implicit presence, behind the scenes, throughout the story. In one sense, she is the archetypal story.

Events have to be as they are. Modern masters of fiction like Henry James speak of the process of starting with a fragment — it may be a character, or even one aspect or trait of a character — and then drawing out the story that is contained within the fragment.[29] Here lies the art, of providing a context in which the seed may germinate. That seed contains everything within. The seed runs the story, like a bolting horse carrying its hapless rider, whose challenge is to stay in the saddle and rein in the horse past hazards blocking its way, until it has exhausted itself and completed its journey.

So it is with the archetype — the *type* that was *en archē*, in the beginning, at the foundation. The seed is the anger of Achilles, who has grief embedded in his name — that is, in his nature. Everything flows from these three things: the man, his rage, and his suffering. Similarly, the archetype of the hero, as made flesh in the story of Achilles, will program all of its later reworkings down through the history of the West, from national war myths to the American Western.

Today, we have no answer to the question of where the archetype came from, or who supplied it. Who sowed the seed? Our strong inclination is to attribute all creative works to a human individual — the author. Yet while we may register the timeless authority of a story like the *Iliad*, we are blind to its formation. The Greeks, led by Homer, were less perplexed.

Homer refers to what is about to be told as 'our story'. By 'our', does he mean the goddess and him? Or her, him, and the listeners? The poet is on intimate terms with the divinity who speaks through him. He is like Achilles standing unarmed on the edge of the battle, his head emanating a far-shining flame, the poet's red-golden flame being his song. The consequence is that for listeners who become engrossed in Homer's story, standing on the edge of the battle themselves, looking on, the goddess is close by.

DELPHI: SANCTUARY VIEWED FROM
TEMPLE OF ATHENA

SIX

THE HERITAGE

What am I claiming?

We breathe culture, and the essential elements of what we breathe were transmitted a long time ago. There is a cultural gene that was planted in the beginning, determining what would follow. But, wait a minute, we should pause here: what is the status of this 'gene' metaphor? Whatever was in the beginning is more than obscure; it is completely unknown. Surely any hypothesis about origins is as good as any other. Positing something definite is as unconvincing, even spurious, as assertions about the nature of God.

What we do have to work with is what came later — the effects, the symptoms. Reading them allows us to project backwards, using a combination of informed speculation and plausible deduction. The process is like medical diagnosis: the patient presents with a range of symptoms, which the doctors chart, and from there proceed, drawing on their training and experience, to make a calculated guess as to the underlying disease — the first cause which produced the symptoms.

Put differently, what results in this quest for origins has the status of an 'as if' statement. It is *as if* it was like this in the beginning. The hypothesis about origins makes sense of what followed, and of the historical path the culture took as it evolved. It helps us better understand that path.

Not that the beginning was like infancy, the start of the long development to maturity — here, 'evolution' is a false metaphor. In the beginning, the culture was fully formed, like Athena at her birth, her adult self springing fully clad and armed from her father's head. Perhaps this is the deep truth about her legendary birth: wisdom comes into the world complete. At most, some details remain to be filled in later.

With cultural archetypes, continuity reigns: the past is continually reworked and elaborated. In weak periods there is forgetting and denial, leading into a failure to rise above the pedestrian routines and necessities of everyday life. Remembering is vital. To bring the significant past back to life is to illuminate the present, animating it.

The alternative view about cultural formation holds that randomness rules. Individuals are formed by a chance mix of genes at conception, and born accidentally into a particular society and into particular times. The only continuities are those of habit, custom, and institutional rigidity — all of which may be overturned by new generations, if what they inherit does not suit their tastes. Human reality is socially constructed; its truths are relative, not absolute.

A major problem with this view is that very few people — only a small fraction of the modern intelligentsia — have ever thought in such terms. The norm is for individuals to fashion plausible stories to give shape and sense to their lives; and those stories seem inevitably to place weight on a significant past that prepares the way for the present, and may direct them into the future. Furthermore, the body of publicly told stories that people draw upon, to help imagine their own narratives, repeats age-old motifs; and the cardinal moral laws they try to live by are the same, with few exceptions, as those which prevailed in fifth-century-BC Athens. Some things are socially constructed, and peculiar to a particular time and place, but not the forms that matter.

If the significant past does not shape what follows — if it is merely an obsolete curiosity — we humans would be condemned to a dreary arbitrariness, imprisoned in the present. We would be trapped in the self, at best passing the time while distracted by ephemeral pleasures. This is the life of the Lotus Eaters, whom Odysseus encounters: the plant acts as a drug, making those who taste it lose all sense of time, and forget the way home. From individuals to sporting clubs to societies as a whole, those who fail to venerate past generations, and their achievements, will fail to take responsibility for the next generation. To care for those who came before is to care for those still to come. Children gain a love for the world they inherit in good part because of stories they have heard about how it was built. And we humans seem inwardly driven to tell stories about the heroic past.

Put bluntly, why do we bother about the past? Why treasure the ruins — why not just travel to five-star hotels set beside tropical beaches? Why continue to read Homer, Sophocles, and Plato? Why keep returning to neo-classical forms in architecture? Even that Mecca of contemporary entertainment, Las Vegas, centres on casinos that have as their major attraction the extravagant simulation of the past — the most famous of them all, *Caesar's*

Palace, an American simulation of a Roman simulation of classical Greek forms.

Why are we haunted by some music? It is because it takes us beyond time and place, into a grander realm where no clock ticks, and no boundaries constrain us. It is as if it rises out of some vast, enchanted past, and transmits to us, obscurely, the tune of eternity, carrying us away with it. Ancient Greece made music for the Western ear.

In fact, the origin I am positing is less obscure than that of a pure 'as if' hypothesis. The origin is Homer, elaborated over three centuries from 700 BC to 400 BC, reaching its completion in Athens. Those three centuries saw the establishment of Delphi and Olympia;[1] the highpoint of Greek sculpture and tragedy; the birth of Greek mathematics and philosophy; and the building of the Parthenon and the Erechtheion.

The two temples represent the driving dynamic that emerges. Looking one way, there is the exhilaration of perfect form shining in the luminous, blue, early-morning Athenian air. It inspires ambition and striving. It evokes the stance of Achilles: invincible, huge and splendid on the edge of the battle; the sublime, timeless poise of the Delphic charioteer; and the confidence to build a civilisation. Looking the other way, there is brooding, glowering disapproval, cautioning us to take care and not to get too carried away. Yet the Karyatids are just as enchanting as the Parthenon. Something in their look charms us, drawing the fearful passer-by closer, fascinated and appalled, suspecting that to turn away would be to turn away from life itself.

The thesis of this book is that Western culture is created out of the tension between Shining and dark saying; it is generated from the electric current flashing between these two poles.

What was it that made those ancient Greeks so magisterial and imposing, so vital and clear-sighted — so superior? Was it through knowing that a god was near, but difficult to grasp? Something like this awareness seems to lurk behind the enigmatic smile of those archaic Greek faces, worked in stone, their look intimate and full on, but distant, as if belonging to an eternity beyond, yet present — that discerning look taking in their human opposites, both the now of the mortal life and the forever (see p. 118 for a later example). And also lurking there is the compounding knowledge that, close by, dark voices murmured. The hook-taloned maid of the riddling speech gazed on with disdain, posing Apollo's question to every passer-by: 'Who are you?' Indeed, 'Who are you?' To have no answer is death.

Once set, this culture proceeded on its path to us, projecting an image of our ideal self. It was concocted from a volatile mix of fatalism, scepticism, and confidence. All three fuse in the warning, 'Remember that you are not a god' — its signal to us, in negation, that these people were so confident that they could imagine themselves as godlike, and needed to check themselves in their vanity.

Nietzsche attributed to those Greeks a wonderful combination of hair-raising cheerfulness with gratitude.[2] Knowing the darkest possibilities, they faced them square on, impatient with redeeming illusions of progress, of rebirth, and of the transformation of self into something stronger and better; and preferring gods that were capricious, but sometimes generous, over those that consoled and saved. It is as if, in scorning the illusions that protect everyday life from sinking into absurdity, they found a zest and buoyancy. It is as if the very act of staring clear-eyed into the Karyatid darkness lifted the spirits, making these Greeks accepting of life, even grateful for it, and reverent. The paradox was that here was a people who found despair to be enabling, predestination to be liberating, and tragedy to be exhilarating.

If ancient Greece laid the foundations, what followed? What was the aftermath? What were the consequences? At issue is the metaphysical history of the West.

After Alexander the Great comes Jesus. Mark, the first to write the story of his life, reworks the Greek *mythos*. While the narrative is informed by the Jewish scriptures, Mark shifts away from monotheism to the polytheism of the godlike hero, combined with teachings about *pneuma* (a sacred breath, wind or spirit). The fourth and last to write the story, John, underlines this shift.[3]

Jesus marks a new direction, and yet doesn't. Whatever is divine on the human plane is located in the living individual, its blueprint in the exemplary man. This Jesus is at war with his own culture, with Jewish monotheism. He asserts, as his central teaching: 'I am.' With these two words he explicitly countermands the God of the Hebrew Bible, who had proclaimed his identity to Moses: 'I am that I am'. Jesus replaces him. As John puts it in his prologue: 'All things came through him, and without him nothing was made, that has come into being. In him was life, and the life was the light of men.' Genesis is rewritten: the new Creation opens with the *word*, or the *story* — and the story is that of Jesus. It is his individual being that lies at the core of the mystery — not God's. The ancient Greeks provided the precedent, in their own historical lineage: the age of the gods was replaced by the age of the heroes, led by Achilles; and it was followed, in turn, by the age of ordinary mortals.

While Jesus does supersede the Jewish God, his more intriguing relationship is with Athena. The affinities are much closer. In effect, she is metamorphosed into him and his story. He walks on the Sea of Galilee in the middle of the night, terrifying his followers, who take him to be a phantasm. He shines with a gleaming, white radiance during his Transfiguration on the mountain, as Mark describes it, at the exact midpoint of the story. Jesus plunges into the Karyatid dark during his agony in the night garden, a garden of olives. The story ends with a young man in white sitting inside an empty tomb, telling the reader not to be alarmed — a surreal young man reminiscent of one of the guises taken by Athena when she appears to Odysseus. Further, the 'godlike' in Jesus borrows from some of the deep wisdom attributed to the Greek goddess. If Apollo is a ritual antagonist of Achilles, because the hero is in the process of replacing the god, then Athena would have the same grounds for hostility to Jesus. He supersedes her.

The Jesus of Mark and John is, equally, a radical midrash of *godlike* Achilles. Jesus represents a different type of warrior, but this is a superficial contrast. Both are profoundly solitary individuals, men of sorrows burdened by their tragic destinies. Both learn through suffering. Both teach through the example of their life-story, rather than by means of anything they say. Both are illuminated in transcendental golden light at the critical midpoint in their life, the moment at which each steps into the tragic last phase of his mission. Both achieve a terrible, charismatic grandeur once they have moved into the shadow of their impending death — a fated death, which they see clearly, rushing towards them. The continuity is underlined in that both Mark and John wrote in Greek, and both are masterly in their use of the language — *pneuma* is a recurring presence in both texts.

From the outset, the Christian church set about restoring the monotheistic God pictured in what it labelled the 'Old Testament'. Hellenism as the formative culture of the West gave way to Christianity. On the larger historical stage, the Romans engineered the change, switching from their own cardboard imitation of Greek culture to an imperial form of monotheism. Emblematic of the shift, it was a crusading Christian Roman emperor, Theodosius I, who closed down the sanctuary at Olympia, in AD 393, in an anti-pagan purge, thus bringing the twelve-hundred-year run of the ancient Games to an end. He also closed down the Delphic Oracle.

Christianity thereby led the West into a long, circuitous regression that would last for nearly two millennia. Monotheism is in conflict with the defining Western strengths, and at odds with the West's characteristic virtues, the source of its vitality: a rugged individualism, focused on acting in the world here and now; a sceptical, inquiring orientation; a counterbalancing, soulful, reflective inwardness; a conception of metropolitan living, with the civic sphere conducted according to democratic principles; and a concern with adorning the human domain with acts and things of beauty. To project divinity way beyond all this, into a great and unbridgeable distance, and to inflate its power, was to devalue the human world.

What I am proposing is that the metaphysical history of the West begins in ancient Greece, with the paradigm scripted by Homer, then elaborated in fifth-century Athens. It reaches its climax in the figure of Jesus. Jesus marks a radical junction, an either-or that might have gone either way. Here is the fateful turning point in Western history.[4] Paul's driving, messianic Puritanism, in conjunction with Matthew's revisionist story of Jesus's life, spawns Christianity, the religion built in Jesus's name. Christianity then proceeds to plunge the West into centuries of dogmatic torpor.[5]

The Renaissance marked the start of the move back to recover what had been lost, inaugurating a long and slow process that would continue for five hundred years. By the twentieth century, the West had largely thrown off the stifling cloak of monotheism; but, at the same time, it found itself bewildered and disenchanted. This is another story, one centring on the modern failure, in the wake of the death of the singular God, to bring back to life what Athena and Jesus once represented. Out of disenchantment, following the loss of the *mythos,* the West has taken the alternative way, that of Socrates. It has embraced Socrates as its consoling messiah. Again, it is the ancient Greeks who provide the cultural map: Socrates versus Athena and Jesus.

The Socratic consolation is the redeeming illusion that humans are free — and fundamentally, not trivially free. The crux of human 'freedom' is the potential in individuals to change themselves and their conditions. The West has proved this to be possible, and spectacularly so, at the social, economic, and institutional level. Not so with individuals, however, in the realm of metaphysics — the realm in which the Athenian philosopher led them to believe that it is possible, through thinking, to reform being.[6] Just as the French Revolution, which itself chose Socrates as its founding prophet, enacted a very different and terror-ridden reality to the one it had promised — an Enlightened age of 'liberty, equality, and fraternity' — so, too, the Socratic mode for the modern Western individual produced a two-headed pathology. One head evaded 'Know thyself', losing itself in cloudy dreams of the person it might turn into ... if only. The other turned angrily towards the world, displacing anxiety into rancour, blaming others for its unhappy state, and snarling with righteous indignation at those who were less afflicted.

Western religion has come in three forms: monotheism, in the Judaeo-Christian mode; Greek polytheism, with its powerful later sublimated forms; and *pneuma* religion, hinging on the belief that a sacred breath or divine spirit permeates the world. Let me dwell briefly on the heritage of polytheism and pneuma religion.

What were the key components of Greek polytheism that have endured? There was the ideal of *euruthmia*, 'beautiful rhythm', which has re-emerged in the modern West. The assumption was that the vital human task is religious: to find earthly means for contact with the gods. This is best done through individuals creating their own timeless representations of the divine. Human excellence may capture the shapes of the sacred. Ancient Greek culture provides much of the Western blueprint for precisely this endeavour: in oratory; in dramatic epic and tragedy; in architecture and sculpture; in mathematical theorems; and in athletic festivals, which were conceived as religious. In the modern Olympic Games, which is one of the most successful Greek revivals, virtuosity of performance is celebrated — from the sheer physical power and fleetness of the sprint, to the sublime grace of high-board diving, to the elegance of equestrian show-jumping. Billions of people around the world watch all this on television.

This ideal of human excellence, which was established by Homer, instructs us that the most important focus of life is the transcendental act: individuals finding a way of acting in the world that is so awesome and exemplary that they become larger than their ordinary, clumsy, everyday selves. In this sublime moment, they become vehicles mediating earth and heaven. Homer repeatedly characterises the quintessential hero, Achilles, as 'godlike', which means that he transcends his mortal self through what he does, and through who he is.

The transcendental act is the supreme religious experience. The Greeks, again led by Homer, often describe the experience, both for the actor and those observing, as being one in which a god breathes through the hero, or bathes him in divine radiance. Today, when we use the word 'inspired', surely we are not imagining anything very different. The spirit moves; the god possesses. Homer evoked this sublime experience with luminous narrative flair.

Athena's *nearness* shades into the image, more credible in our modern eyes, of her lifting the hero's spirits and bathing him in her golden light. Here, we move closer to the view of 'sacred pneuma', a breath of divinity that may surround, and even possess, mortals in moments of inspiration. Such a view of pneuma becomes explicit in the later philosophical school of Greek Stoicism. Later again, in his Life of Jesus, John will famously evoke sacred pneuma as 'the wind that bloweth where it wills, and thou hearest its sound, but canst not tell whence it cometh, and whither it goeth.'[7]

Polytheism is another way of saying that *mythos* depends on larger-than-life forms. It follows that polytheism is the religious norm, for all cultures and in all times. This norm will always resurface amongst humans. And, in the West, this is precisely what has happened since the Renaissance. The gods have been sublimated into secular icons and heroes. The Renaissance was a rebirth of Greek polytheism in sublimated forms. The secular icons include Michelangelo's David, the Mona Lisa, Raphael's Madonnas,[8] Rembrandt's self-portraits, Joan of Arc, Nelson's Column, and the Statue of Liberty. It is telling that the Statue of Liberty is clad in Greek robes. Mathematical discoveries and their scientific derivatives, continuing the Greek heritage, have once again come to be accorded Platonic status: the laws of gravity, the theories of evolution and relativity, DNA, and various inventions from the steam engine to the microchip. The list of heroes (and they are not 'saints') includes Leonardo, Shakespeare, Newton, Kant, Mozart, Goethe, Napoleon, Darwin, Abraham Lincoln, and Winston Churchill. Is not Marilyn Monroe a secular projection of Aphrodite? Elvis Presley, a hybrid reincarnation of Orpheus and Pan? In the classical descending hierarchy of gods, heroes, and mortals, the gods and the heroes have been conflated into a single category. Meanwhile, the singular, all-powerful Christian God has disappeared from the scene.

Pneuma religion has returned writ large in the West since the rise of Romanticism in the eighteenth century. It focuses, in its modern guise, on losing the self in higher inspiration, and going to places in which the spirit is more likely to be near. The contemporary Westerner finds the ideal escape from work and the city in Nature: whether it is at leisure on beaches, breathing in the expanses of ocean and sea; or bushwalking and cycling; or fishing alone in the early dawn, meditating on the vastness of water and heaven; or playing golf, cocooned in an oasis of green; or picnicking in woods, up mountains, or by streams.

Then there is the swoon of romance. The predominant forms of modern entertainment, apart from sport, are the Hollywood film, the television soap-opera, and popular music. Within all three, the most common story is the romance. The stock motif has the couple swept off their feet, as if they have breathed an intoxicating drug that has carried them into some enchanted place all of their own. The atmospherics are those of unadulterated pneuma.

The modern sporting crowd exemplifies the return of the classical Greek religious vision. Sporting stadiums, today's counterparts to medieval cathedrals, dot the Western world. Within them, a type of secular worship is taking place. The match, conducted on the 'sacred turf', inspires collective mania. Waves of sound, like that of a deep, primitive chant, erupt from tens of thousands of voices ululating as one, singing, groaning, and exulting in their euphoria, their anxiety, and their despair. Alcohol inflames drunken emotions, like in an ancient Dionysian festival. Equally, drink sedates the anguish of those supporting the losing side. Classical Greek theatre is reborn here, with the crowd performing as the ancient chorus.

These modern half-secular, half-sacred festivals flourish because of what excites the crowds, drawing them in, and inducing them to shed most of their normal inhibitions: the spectacle of teams of athletes in deadly serious competition. Each one of those athletes strives to perform in the superhuman, larger-than-life image of the hero, as it has flowed on down through the Western tradition from its origin in Achilles. It may not be entirely fanciful to note that the modern mega-stadium has almost identical external dimensions to those of the ancient city of Troy, with one detail reversed: the Trojans, standing on the ramparts, looked outwards from the city walls, down at armour-clad Hektor running three times around them, pursued by Achilles, whereas the modern fan looks inwards, down from on high, at athletes speeding around the central arena.

Nevertheless, the return of the ancient Greek religious vision is not complete. It can never function as it once did until there is a recovery of what Athena and Jesus represented.

The classical Greek heritage is to be traced throughout Western life. But just as significant as the mark of its blueprint on modern ways is what survives in Greece itself. This book was born out of travelling in Greece today. The journey charmed. It was being there that, to borrow Joseph Conrad's way of putting it, switched the glamour on.

To complete the metaphysical journey, I want to return to the actual journey. Charm depends on impressions that cue and awaken sub-conscious traces — glow-worms of emotional intensity that, once switched on, do not fade. As jewels of enduring significance that brighten the soul, they haunt the deeper imagination. There is a technique for recovering such traces, requiring a special kind of reflection: putting oneself into a semi-trance state, and seeing which images rise out of this sea of dreams, and wash over one. Freud called a similar technique 'free association'.

I am on the road from Thebes to Delphi, approaching where the three ways met. The way is bleak; the lower slopes of the mountain, rocky and inhospitable, uninviting. I sense somewhere close by the presence of that monstrous stalker, the hook-taloned maid of the riddling speech, lying in wait. She tracks us all. I imagine Oedipus up ahead, approaching fast, descending the mountain at a frenzied pace, pursued by the Furies and the dread memory of his moment with the Pythian Oracle, his mind quaking with images of what happened there inside the *adyton* — her chanted refrain, crooning seductively yet dispassionately the terror that might become his life. This man has been stripped of all his characteristic self-assurance and composure. His words, in answer to the riddle soon to be put to him, will be as nothing, a flutter in the wind, next to what he has just been told — and anyone who is impressed by him as the smartest of men should check themselves, think again, and bow down before the real power: oracular Delphi.

His weeks waiting up there for his call had been tinged with fearful anticipation. On edge, he had yet managed to let the site work its mystery. I imagine him as a spectator at the Pythian Games.

I see him strolling up the narrow, winding, sacred way, pushing through the dense throng of visitors, taking in the fabulously decorated, richly stocked treasuries, and the hundreds of statues, the huge Apollo, and the Sphinx of Naxos.

I see him seated high up in the amphitheatre, gazing far out across the Delphi landscape glistening in its ethereal light, listening to hymns to Apollo rising up from the stage far below, spicing the mountain air; I imagine him later, on the same stone bench, engrossed in tragic drama, blind to his own future place as the doomed hero on this very stage, his life to be mimed by unknowing others (see p. 178). In the stadium, set privately in woods at the top of the sanctuary precinct, he finds a simpler pleasure watching chariot-races — sport is so uncomplicated. Mainly, though, I imagine him forbiddingly alone, unable to speak to another soul — for what could he say, cast as he has been far beyond small-talk? He withdraws into his solitariness to brood, as he steels himself and breathes in the enigma.

On the appointed day — it was only yesterday — the priests, standing at the top of the entrance ramp, under the emblematic E of being, welcomed him to Apollo's Temple. They escorted him through the foyer, gesturing in passing to the two chiselled mottos, 'Know thyself!' and 'Nothing in excess!' They led him into the temple proper, the *megaron*, where he was humbled by the vast space, making out in the dim light the sanctuary of Poseidon behind columns off to the right, with the Pythia's private domain off to the left. Proceeding through the long stretch of the middle nave to the rear, he was directed down some steps, smoke stinging his eyes, the strong whiff of burning laurel irritating his nose, to be sat against the back wall of a confined private chamber.

In flickering lamplight, through a colonnade that separated

him from the seat of pronouncement, there she was. He could just make her out in the murky haze — the most famous, infamous, and yet nameless woman in the world. Dressed in a simple white tunic, her face deathly pale, her long hair wild, she was seated on a bronze tripod, a ghostly presence, her bare feet swaying off the ground. There she was, the prophetic seer, the third of the Fates, perched in her sacred lair, exuding mystic potency, surrounded by her totems: the Omphalos stone marking this spot as the god-decreed navel of the earth, the centre of human existence; a gold figurine of Apollo; an altar with burning bay branches; and a small fountain with water trickling into an urn. Pungent chemical vapours blended with the laurel and bay smoke, making him light-headed and slightly nauseous.

His memory now, as he lurches and stumbles down the track towards the three ways, is like his vision then — jumpy and blurred. Were those eyes fixed coldly on him, before they glazed over? Was that a thin, bemused smile, before she began to moan? Was that mocking pity in her voice, as she chanted out his destiny? All of his horror is condensed into the memory of that voice — it is as if she was only a disembodied voice, and everything else inside the Temple was a fleeting mirage. The god had taken over. The sound now jamming his ears is incantatory, musical but without harmony: rasping sharp, the words nailing him to Necessity, piercing through to the entrails of meaning.

I am on the plains of Troy, near the Greek ships, with battle raging around. I see a man appear, alone, huge and splendid, unarmed, his head and shoulders radiated in golden light. He bellows out a great cry. Pealing over the warring men is his grief and his rage, like rolling thunder punctuated with three deafening claps. The Trojans, and even his fellow Greeks, too, shiver with the ominous threat of the brute man-slaughtering havoc that his entry into the fighting is about to unleash. I see him clad in his shining god-crafted armour, sprinting after Hektor, three times around the walls of Troy, the citizens above looking down, terrified. Andromache, Hektor's doomed wife, labours obliviously deep inside the fortress, drawing a hot bath for the husband who is about to die, she herself an automaton, just keeping herself busy, trying to repress nightmare images of her own impending slavery and the murder of her little son. And Hektor is such a pitiful sight that the onlooker has to turn away at the shame of this man who was, until a moment ago, supreme among Trojan warriors, and is now but a frightened coward.

Achilles sprints in vengeance after the killer of Patroklos. But the hero belongs half among the divinities and a swarm of forces that move in the beyond. So what he pursues around the walls of Troy is not really Hektor, but his own doom; he is a man driven to catch his fate, wrap his arms around it in a firm embrace, and bring it on. His grief, instead of flattening him, has pitched him into a love affair with death. A type of erotic warmth rises within him, like bright-green moss flourishing under a dank twilight shadow, paradoxical, feeding his courtesy, his poise, and his peerless gentlemanly aura.

I see that same man, later, welcoming the enemy king into his dwelling, addressing him, 'Aged, magnificent sir!', serving him food and wine, and weeping together with him at the pity of it all, the futility and the nobility, the pettiness and the suffering and the gravity. The two big men become friends.

I am strolling among the ruins at Olympia. It is a relief to be here. Sport is not war. The hub is the Temple of Zeus, with massive columns lying beside it, toppled by earthquakes in AD 551 and

AD 552 — a colossus flattened as if by gods mocking their titanic, insubstantial hubris. *Who do they think they are, these humans?* Or maybe the gods were signalling their disapproval of that Roman emperor who had closed the site; and of his namesake follower, Emperor Theodosius II, who set fire to the temple. So the great Doric columns have lain for fourteen hundred years.

Or maybe it was quite different. Here is the tomb of the King of the Gods, Zeus: the toppled columns are his limbs, and Olympia is the graveyard of the Hellenistic era in the West. Yet this site has not gone cold, as if it were abandoned and forgotten. The temple is like some awesome, slumbering giant sprawled here, harbouring within an ancient force, pent up, just waiting to be tapped once again — as Pierre de Coubertin discovered. I see the modern Olympic Games, in all its world-conquering might, which even Alexander the Great might have envied, emerging from the tiny kernel treasured here, within the Temple of Zeus at Olympia.

All is ease in Arcadia. I am in another world, breathing in the pervasive calm, entranced by a landscape of serenity and balance. Olympia is what Nicolas Poussin captured in the seventeenth century in his great landscape paintings, in which he integrated humans at work and play into nature — a nature usually undulating, heavily treed, and centring on a lake, flanked by a neo-classical town. Poussin did not know the actual Olympia — although he did refer to Arcadia. It is what, continuing the same tradition, the English landscape designers of the eighteenth century, led by Capability Brown, strove to create in their grand gardens, even to the point of fabricating classical ruins and embedding them strategically in their vistas.

The Arcadian spirit found at Olympia is not typical of ancient Greece. At the Acropolis, Delphi, and Troy — the three

OLYMPIA: TEMPLE OF ZEUS

formative sites — it is only present fitfully, heavily qualified, at best subordinate. To be sure, Athena's temple in Delphi is a quiet corner set amongst olive trees; but what it looks out at, a kilometre away and above, is Apollo's sanctuary, centred on a massive, masculine temple. At Olympia, the Temple of Zeus is also massively masculine, but not overbearing; it blends into the flat, wooded terrain.

The mood at Olympia draws my reflections to Delos. An island far apart, a sanctuary from the harshness of living, it offers a haven. When Odysseus rhapsodises to his long-suffering wife that he has been told that death will come upon him 'mild as air', he signals his true homecoming. His journey is a parable of the life struggle, of the actual human path: ten years at sea hounded by malevolent supernatural forces, blown from one hostile location to the next, with occasional respite, a captain in name, but with very little control over his life. Yet he was the smartest of all tacticians. It is as if, at last, his ship has found the sheltered cove at Delos, has docked, and he has come ashore. His story reminds us that the ancient Greeks were a sea-faring people, and that their experience was ingrained with metaphors of perilous journeys in fragile craft crossing over dark waters, their wellbeing subject to the whim of superhumanly powerful natural forces.

A mellow, kindly Apollo awaits the weary hero at Delos, the god having left his darker female accomplices, the Sphinx and the Pythian Oracle, far away at his other site, Delphi. We may stroll among the ruins with Odysseus, protected from the elements by a semi-circle of hillocks to the rear, the wine-dark sea just beyond the headland, and off in the distance the vista of other mountain-grand islands among the Cyclades — so named from ancient times, the circle (*kuklos*) of islands which surround the centre, sacred Delos.

The memory of these island peaks takes me back to the mainland, to Mt Olympus. I see it snow-capped, unapproachable, and eternally distant (see p. 188). Wherever you travel in northern Greece, there it is, the Archimedean point, the fixed locus by which everywhere else sets its bearings. It is always present in the corner of the mind; like its physical reality, it is huge and difficult to get around, an almost impassable titanic monolith, its immortal substantiality casting it outside time, as if it were here when the world began, and will continue exactly as it is, forever, even if the world ends. Do the gods indeed dwell up there, in the home they always return to like sacred bees swarming to an invisible hive? Mt Olympus has one unambiguous message for those who pass below: the gods are near, but difficult to grasp.

Alexander the Great was born just behind Mt Olympus, to the north, growing up under its shadow, taught there by Aristotle. Maybe its massive aura set the trajectory of the superhuman journey that was Alexander's adult life, in his quest to shape the world to his own towering Olympic vision.

Throughout the Greek journey, one is overwhelmed by the primacy of landscape. Homer's similes, which are without peer — the best we have been given — inspire a sensual reverence for the beauty of nature. The landscape dwarfs us mortals, and not just in its extreme versions, which Greece nurtures, from earthquakes to storms at sea. It renders us puny, in space and time, but simultaneously offers a means by which we can make ourselves more substantial. Homer shows us how, by drawing on its example: his use of simile is a means for imbibing nature's dynamism, and for emulating its majesty. To choose two images from hundreds, virtually at random:

As when the west wind strikes in the deepening
whirlstorm to batter the clouds of the shining south wind,
so that the bulging big waves roll hard and the blown spume
scatters high before the force of the veering wind's blast.
So the massed high heads of the people were struck down by Hektor.[9]

... the son of Peleus rose like a lion against him,
the baleful beast, when men have been straining to kill him, the county
all in the hunt, and he at the first pays them no attention
but goes his way, only when some one of the impetuous young men
has hit him with the spear he whirls, jaws open, over his teeth foam
breaks out, and in the depths of his chest the powerful heart groans;
he lashes his own ribs with his tail and the flanks on both sides
as he rouses himself to fury for the fight, eyes glaring,
and hurls himself straight onward on the chance of killing some one
of the men, or else being killed himself in the first onrush.
So the proud heart and fighting fury stirred on Achilleus.[10]

Hektor and Achilles become 'forces of nature'.

I am approaching Mycenae. The mood is set from afar, from first sight of this fortress, fashioned as if by a one-eyed giant Cyclops, of huge, grey, raw-chiselled boulders. Grey, massive, and oppressive, the mood only darkens as one gets closer and then begins the final approach to the Lion Gate. The road up to the entrance passes between claustrophobia-inducing granite walls towering eight metres high on either side, the way today remaining just as it would have been three thousand years ago when Kassandra, enslaved, descended from Agamemnon's chariot, trembling and choking on what she foresaw, and began her slow walk along the royal-blue carpet 'to take her fate'. Strangely, this is the only part of the fortress that remains largely intact — Kassandra's gate, as one might call it (see p. 53).

I see Kassandra standing here. At first sight, she appears as a scantily clad girl, brought to a chillingly alien place, surrounded by people who either scorn her in her degradation or hate her. She crouches wild-eyed, panicked, like a cornered cat, her fright turning into hysteria. Yet, as she gathers herself, she is formidable. It is easy to understand Apollo's infatuation with her: there was her beauty, of course, and her chaste aloofness. But there was more to it: he saw that, in her, he had met his human match. The god came near, and she was not afraid; looking him coolly in the eye, she said 'No.' In resisting him, she confirmed the powers they shared: the knowledge of the deep mysteries, including the future, and the power of music — her song carrying all the beauty of the nightingale, but deeper, for its refrain was the tragedy of being born human, and seeing with radiant clarity the truth of what was and of what would be.

The ancient story refers to Kassandra being brought to Mycenae as Agamemnon's slave concubine, an item of booty he seized from the fall of Troy.[11] But it is impossible to conceive of this man touching her — he, the one with brutal appetites, a sordid mania for power, and a petulant, cowardly envy of Achilles, who was the better man by far. Even Agamemnon, in his swarthy, thick-necked insensitivity, would not dare come close, lest he burn. I see in a different way, too, the murderous rage flaming in the heart of Queen Klytemnestra as she welcomed King Agamemnon home, and invited him to enter the palace by impiously treading the royal-blue carpet. The rage was not fired by hatred of her husband; she knew him all too well for that. It was, rather, envy of Kassandra that unhinged her. It would be difficult for anyone — indeed, dreadful — to be in the presence of the woman whom the god bowed down before, she who described her fate as the 'sheer edge of the tearing iron'. If those far-seeing eyes, which dwelt in the beyond, focused on eternity, selected you for an instant, and shone on you, here and now, how would you withstand their gaze? Klytemnestra and her husband were both woefully unworthy, and knew it.

Today, while the Mycenaean palace is just a tourist site, the ghosts of events that took place three millennia ago still hang in the air, creating a canopy of unsettling horror brooding overhead, pressing visitors to clear out. Kassandra saw crowding here a 'drunken rout of ingrown vengeful spirits'. Some traces endure, urging visitors not to linger lest some of the blood-thick pollution infect them.

I am in Athens in the early morning, having just flown in. Walking up the winding ascent from the Plaka area directly beneath the Acropolis, I pass the rocky outcrop of the Areopagus on the right, and come out on the level parking-area opposite the main gate. Instead of climbing the Acropolis directly, I keep walking past the entrance, through olives, along the road that descends towards the south. It is the access road for visitors' cars and buses, and runs off one of the major avenues in Athens. I cross the avenue and take a track that rises through thick pine woods to the west. Following it past a Greek Orthodox church, and climbing, I soon come out at a wide expanse of rock-based open ground, softened by areas of grass. The land, on two levels, is large enough to accommodate six thousand people. It drops away precipitously in front, down into a valley. In the distance are suburbs. This is the Pnyx.

The ancient Athenians assembled here to debate affairs of state and to vote on them. It is the birth-site of democracy, where the locals displayed themselves at their best and their worst. The art of oratory and rhetoric, as we know it in the West, originated here, cultivated by the need, in a leader as in an ordinary citizen, to bring the majority around to his point of view. At the same time, it was the location where the assembly started the annual ostracism process, which resulted in citizens voting to banish prominent contemporaries to a ten-year exile from Attika. While initially introduced as a check on tyranny, the process turned, in practice, into institutionalised rancour. Three of Athens' great fifth-century leaders were victims of ostracism: Themistokles, Kimon, and Aristides the Just.

The Pnyx is not self-contained; it is not the source of its own authority. To the right, exposed to full view, five hundred metres away, and above, like a revelation, is the Parthenon (see p. 180). The perspective from here gives the impression of the temple hovering, the west face front on, sitting on top of the mass of the Acropolis rock, the accumulation of entrance buildings including the Propylaia forming its indistinct base. The angle of sight means that the front plane of the Parthenon slants slightly backwards, making the building appear oriented as much towards the heavens as the earth, and to stand inaccessibly aloof. The Pentelic marble is radiant white; and the perfect sculptured whole — of columns, entablature, and triangular pediment — is framed, halo-like, by the shimmering, blue, early-morning Mediterranean light. The transcendent form is near, but difficult to grasp.

The Parthenon presides over Athens and its democracy,

reminding the citizens below, by its Shining example, to be artful in their rhetoric, balanced in their deliberations, and wise in their decisions. Such civic virtue is one dimension of being born human, one dimension of the ideal of excellence — which, generalised, exhorts each and every individual to devote themselves to creating right forms and sublime rhythms.

The Parthenon is, in its transcendent mode, the mind of god. It proclaims the empire of *sōphrosunē*. Balance reigns. To sit alone on the Pnyx today, gazing up at the Parthenon, is to be reconnected to the ancient Greece that is closest to the way we aspire to live: that of fifth-century-BC Athens.

The Parthenon is best viewed from the Pnyx. Perikles may well have sited it so that it could be seen from here — distinct, face on, and majestic.[12] By comparison, when the viewer stands on top of the Acropolis, it is up too close. The scaffolding of modern restoration is intrusive. And I am reminded that the inside of the temple, as experienced in Perikles' day, would likely have looked ugly to us, dominated as it was by the huge, ostentatious, and graceless statue of Athena Parthenos. Mind you, after modern visitors have wound their way up the steps climbing the Acropolis, and traversed the grand Propylaia, emerging into bright light on the top plateau, they cannot help but be awestruck by the vastly imposing building standing a hundred metres away, on higher ground and to the right, asserting its timeless perfection.

The annual procession carrying the *peplos*, as illustrated in bas-relief on one of the Parthenon friezes, would have proceeded along the left flank of the Parthenon, following the Panathenaic Way, before circling down to the left, and descending to the Erechtheion, where it would have entered a cramped chamber to stop before the eternally burning Sacred Lamp. There, the women would enact the most deeply religious ceremony in ancient Athens: the robing of the archaic wooden statue of Athena Polias in her new cloak. This was an ancient version of secret women's business. That evening, just outside, the citizens would revel all night as they sacrificed a hundred cows on the altar.

Erechtheion, in name the very chthonic one, is deemed enigma. Today, one enters from the west, past Athena's olive tree, what seem like tiny subterranean rooms, as if entering a tomb, a dank stone crypt. What remains are merely shadows — of primitive, pre-Homeric religious forces lurking in the dark, a legendary snake, the monstrous Medusa, the trident imprint in the floor of the raging earthquake and storm god, Poseidon, and the counter-image of Athena in her wooden fetish form, illuminated by an oil lamp.

Easier to grasp, for us, and more accessible, are the guardians: the six Karyatids. They stand immobile, their implacable, stony glowering so intense that they do not need to catch the eye, indifferent as they are to the wayfarer, whom they know they have entranced (as if they were what they are not — mesmerisingly beautiful women). Their tune is introverted, by contrast with that of the Sirens to Odysseus. These women are subtler in their seductive song, and more honest in their menace. In part, this is because of the way they line up, in their six-times-over massed ranks. But it is due more to what is alluded to in their grim look, what they seem to know. Sentinels of warning, of what lies behind and below them, they are the surface manifestations, like fragments of a nightmare remembered on waking, in trauma, wrought out of subterranean fears, carrying fleeting traces of the message.

The power of the Karyatids is illustrated by the failure of the Parthenon to intimidate them. Who else would not be eclipsed, shrunk into a nonentity, by standing alone, side-by-side the pre-eminent majesty of Perikles' answer to Homer, like the impossible challenge for any warrior of being measured next to Achilles on the field of battle? But the Karyatids are undiminished, standing erect and unmoved, as if it is they who are confronted by insubstantial mediocrity. In a war between cultures, the Parthenon and the Karyatids — these two paradigms with their antagonistic charismas — each stand their ground, indomitable.

Both are simple, concentrated, single images that seize the visual mode of knowing, monopolising it, blurring the other senses. They defy any narrative extension of what they are, asserting that time is a mere mask, a superficial fiction. However we elaborate on them — and this book has been just that, an elaboration on them — by the end of the story, they retain their essential irreducibility, the more beguiling because of the journey we've undertaken. Here, on top of the Acropolis, Shining and dark saying reign together.

In the evening, I return to the Pnyx. The Parthenon shines, spotlit in a blaze of warm, yellow light: a brilliant beacon rising in the heavens like a full, ripe moon on a clear night. However, even here I cannot escape Karyatid culture, the other culture, for I hear a sound in the trees behind me, and imagine the *glaux*, the tiny owl perched there, the totemic embodiment of the goddess watching on, gleaming-eyed — the owl of Athena. The tiny hook-beak is like a talon, as if the Sphinx has her claw set in the middle of her flat, squashed, oval face, the claw anchoring the saucer-eyes — the woman-monster bodiless, all head. She has the poised, cool-eyed detachment of a judge. But what kind of judge is it that sits at night, and just watches, silently, so that they who are watched become self-conscious, turning inward, posing to themselves the ever-present and not-yet-answered riddle? It is eerie now, with the Parthenon, over and above, the beacon, counterbalanced by the gleaming eyes alerted somewhere behind in the dark, resting their gaze on the back of my head.

Some fathomless nostalgia brought me here, some *algos nostos*, or pained longing for home. And now those night eyes planted on the back of my head won't go away as I wander on, like Oedipus, mulling over what has been.

Every living, breathing human is an *I* that, when entering a room, imposes its field of force — a presence that emerges as if from the shadows, like Achilles appearing from nowhere, suddenly there, standing on the edge of battle. Vested in the teeming being of that solitary *I* is a phantasmagoria: a many-layered self with its own history, struggling to integrate a here-and-now rough-chiselled character with ancestral voices — echoes from some primeval past, all with their part in this double drama.

It is a double drama enacted on a revolving stage, with one of the sets being the room in which we meet today, and the play being performed like a mask covering the actual face. On the other set, the one staged behind, an eternal *mythos* plays out: the *mythos* explored in the Greek journey taken in this book. On the back stage, too, signs may appear that gods are near — a shout, a flame far-shining. And, most telling of all for the one who has entered the room, there is the script, the invisible net cast over the head — worn lightly, with grace, if the person is fortunate — strung to a silver thread that tugs them forward into the room, to linger for a while, then back out through the door, and away.

It is time to exit with them. My story is told. This has all been seen from afar, like it was the timeless dream that has been my life.

DELPHI: AMPHITHEATRE

PART II

TRAVEL ADVICE

PARTHENON, VIEW FROM PNYX

ONE

FULL JOURNEY (16 DAYS)

INTRODUCTION

To experience the classical Greek world and its ancient sites, as presented in this book, you will need a visit of two weeks or slightly longer. The 16-day itinerary suggested here aims to combine a full range of experience with thoroughness in the particulars, while balancing the intensity of the whole with periods conducted at a more relaxed pace.

I am providing merely the skeleton for the journey, without fleshing out the sort of detail to be found in a guidebook. I prefer to leave to travellers themselves the adventure of planning their daily explorations. Within the skeleton there is room for improvisation, for extending visits in some locations and curtailing the stay in others. Feel, mood, and tone are vital. 'Know thyself' rules Delphi, as it should the wise traveller.

ATHENS — THREE DAYS

The best place to take a hotel in Athens is in the Plaka, directly under the Acropolis. The Plaka is in easy walking distance of the Acropolis, Agora, and surrounds. Also, the area has some charm, a rare quality in this predominantly drab city.

Day 1 — Acropolis

Choose the time of day depending on the season and the density of the tourist throng. In winter, the site shouldn't be too busy at any time; in other seasons, take advice from the hotel on when the Acropolis is likely to be least crowded.

My ideal itinerary

- Starting in the Plaka, walk up the steps and winding path to the Acropolis entrance in the early morning, past the rock of the Areopagus. Continue on past the entrance along the access road, and follow a map to the **Pnyx** 500 metres further on. The view of the Acropolis, and especially the Parthenon, from here, is breathtaking.
- Visit the **Acropolis** itself (morning).
- **Acropolis Museum** (afternoon).
- **Pnyx** (evening)

Day 2

- **National Archaeological Museum** (morning) — allow 2–3 hours.
- **Ancient Agora** and surrounds (afternoon)

Day 3 — Aegina

- Catch the train at Monastiraki *Metro* station to the Piraeus — the ancient and modern port of Athens. Catch a ferry to the island of Aegina (70-minute trip).
- You arrive at Aegina Town. Hire a taxi to visit the **Temple of Aphaia** on the far side of the island. Spend 30 minutes or so there while the taxi waits.
- Return to Athens.
- Buy a road map of Greece and plan the route for days 4–13.

ATHENS-THESSALONIKI-VERGINA-DELPHI — TWO DAYS

Day 4

Hire a car and drive north to **Thessaloniki**, Greece's second-largest city (six hours). The route follows the coast for some of the way, with the large island of Evia on the right. Mt Olympus will feature for the second half of the journey, first appearing ahead, then closer as the road skirts its side, then behind.

The port city of Thessaloniki is far more stylish and cosmopolitan than Athens. Stay there one night.

Day 5

- Early start: drive to **Vergina**, site of the tombs of the ancient royal family of Macedon, including the father of Alexander the Great, Philip II. The tombs were only discovered in 1977, completely undisturbed by robbery or earthquake. As a result, their artefacts are in much better condition than those found in any other ancient Greek archaeological site.

- Set off on the long drive back south. Follow the same route until you reach Kastro, where you take the road to Leivadeia. Alternatively, there is an inland route that leaves the coastal road much earlier, near Thermopyles — I would still suggest taking the route via Leivadeia, so as to approach Delphi on the road from Thebes.
- In Phokis, approaching the beginning of the climb up Mt Parnassus, there is a crossroads, with Daulia marked, off to the right. One-and-a-half kilometres further along the Delphi road there is a carpark on the right. This is possibly where the three roads met, at which Oedipus, descending from Delphi, at a narrow rocky pass, met his father and killed him. (If you are exhausted by now, after a long day, drive past this fateful spot, then return here from Delphi on one of the next three days.)
- Arrive in **Delphi**.

DELPHI — THREE DAYS

Three days is longer than necessary in a strict tourist sense. Delphi has its own atmosphere and mood, and it takes time to acclimatise to it. Also, you will probably need a slower, more relaxed pace after two long, pressured days on the road. In travelling, tempo requires orchestration, with care taken to protect one's psychic energy and receptivity — which depends on not becoming tired and jaded.

Day 6

- **Apollo's Sanctuary–Home of the Oracle**: Allow 2–3 hours with a detailed guidebook, and include the amphitheatre and stadium.

- Explore the town of Delphi and its surrounds. You can walk along goat-tracks circling beneath the town on the steep side of the slope.

Day 7

- **Delphi Museum** (morning)
- Sightseeing drive, back along the road to the next town of Arahova, and take the road to the left which climbs higher up Mt Parnassus (afternoon).

Day 8

- **Temple of Athena**

This serene, detached corner of ancient Delphi is worth several visits. It is especially beautiful in the late afternoon.

OLYMPIA — TWO DAYS

Day 9

Drive from Delphi down the mountain to the port of Itea, then round the picturesque road heading west along the north coast of the Gulf of Corinth to the ancient port city of Naupactos (in Venetian times named Lepanto — the Venetians defeated the Turks near here in a decisive naval battle). From Naupactos continue to Antirio/Rio and take the bridge crossing over the Gulf to the Peloponnese. Continue west to the city of Patras. I recommend avoiding the fast modern highway from Patras to Olympia (a dull route). Rather, take the back-road to Olympia due south through the fertile and mountainous region of Achaia, bordering the fabled Arcadia.

Day 10

- **Olympia Sanctuary** (morning)
- **Olympia Museum** (late morning/early afternoon)
- Drive south to the port city of Kalamata.

SPARTA — ONE DAY

Day 11

- Drive from Kalamata to **Sparta**.
- Sparta is most interesting for its natural location, in a wide, broad valley flanked by towering mountains. It is a spectacular, and fertile location — not at all 'Spartan'. The ruins of ancient Sparta, located on the edge of the modern city, are worth a brief visit.
- Drive to **Nauplion**.

NAUPLION-EPIDAUROS-MYCENAE — TWO DAYS

Day 12

- **Epidauros**

The amphitheatre at Epidauros is extraordinary, with acoustic qualities that have never been matched, either in the ancient or the modern worlds. At different times of year, classical Greek plays are put on in the evenings in the amphitheatre. If there is the opportunity to attend an Aeschylus, Sophocles, or Euripides tragedy, or an Aristophanes comedy here, it is worth rearranging the overall itinerary to fit in.

Day 13

- **Mycenae** (morning)
- Drive back to Athens. Once past Corinth, the freeway flanks the coast, passing the Island of Salamis, and the narrows where the Athenian navy defeated a much larger force of Persian ships in 480 BC.

MYKONOS-DELOS — THREE DAYS

Day 14

- Take a fast ferry from Piraeus to **Mykonos** (3 hours).

Day 15

- Take the early ferry from Mykonos to **Delos** (30 minutes). *Warning*: in winter the Delos ferries may not be running.
- Return to Mykonos.
- Ferry from Mykonos back to Athens.

Day 16

- Depart Athens

GUIDES AND READING

There are excellent guides for do-it-yourself travellers. In my experience, the best current one is the *Lonely Planet* general guide to Greece. It has well-informed coverage of sites and places, including cultural and historical referencing. It is usually reliable in its lists and assessment of accommodation and eating. It also provides useful distance and transport information.

Intensive travelling does not leave much time for incidental reading. On this journey, Sophocles' play *Oedipus the King* will serve as an evocative companion to Delphi. For Mycenae, there is Aeschylus's play *Agamemnon*. For Athens, there is Perikles' Funeral Oration, included in Thucydides *History of the Peloponnesian War*; an Aristophanes comedy, say *Lysistrata*; and a dialogue of Plato describing Socrates at work in the streets of the city, say the *Symposium*.

MOUNT OLYMPUS

TWO

SHORT JOURNEY (8 DAYS)

ATHENS — TWO DAYS

Days 1 and 2

- as for the Full Journey

DELPHI — TWO DAYS

Day 3

- Drive from Athens via Thebes to Delphi
- Sanctuary of Apollo

Day 4

- Delphi Museum
- Temple of Athena

OLYMPIA — TWO DAYS

Day 5

- Drive from Delphi, via Naupactos and Patras to Olympia.
- Olympia Sanctuary (afternoon)

Day 6

- Olympia Museum (morning)
- Drive from Olympia direct, through Arcadia, to Nauplion

EPIDAUROS-MYCENAE — TWO DAYS

Day 7

- Epidauros (morning)
- Mycenae (afternoon)
- Drive directly from Mycenae back to Athens

Day 8

- Depart Athens

NOTES

1. Born into Pilgrimage

1 Plato, *Crito*, 44a.

2 For an account of Byron's Greek pilgrimage see Ruprecht, *Was Greek Thought Religious?*

3 Pausanias, vol. 2, pp. 212–14.

4 The high Mycenaean period lasted from around 1450 BC, with expanding trade and prosperity, until around 1200 BC when fire destroyed the Palace, the Cult Centre, and many other buildings on the citadel. Construction of the fortified citadel had begun around 1350 BC (Spatheri, pp. 18–19). Modern scholars are of the view that the Trojan War, as described by Homer, took place around 1200 BC, towards the end of the Mycenaean Empire.

5 Johann Huizinga, *The Waning of the Middle Ages*, trans. F. Hopman, Penguin, London, 1955.

2. The Acropolis in Athens

1 Hurwit, *The Athenian Acropolis*, p. 166.

2 Shearer, p. 33.

3 Ione Mylonas Shear, 'Kallikrates', *Hesperia*, vol. 32, n. 4, Oct. 1963, p. 410.

4 M. Paton (ed.), *The Erechtheon*. Leicester B. Holland speculates that the Porch of the Maidens, as it has often been called in English, was built to stop rain flooding through a small south door and down stairs into the temple ('Erechtheum Papers IV', *American Journal of Archaeology*, vol. 28, no. 4, 1924, p. 429).

Robin Francis Rhodes reproduces the Paton plan (pp. 132–3). Hurwit agrees about the existence of a door into the temple, while drawing on a later speculative plan of the building by Hans R. Goette (*The Acropolis in the Age of Pericles*, p. 73).

5 Kerenyi, p. 53.

6 Hurwit, *The Acropolis in the Age of Pericles*, pp. 118–21.

7 Rhodes, p. 78.

8 Bertrand Russell, *Mysticism and Logic*, Allen & Unwin, London, 1917, ch. 4.

9 C. J. Herington, pp. 59–67.

10 The term 'civil religion' was coined by Robert Bellah ('Civil Religion in America', *Daedalus*, Winter, 1967).

11 Hurwit, *The Acropolis in the Age of Pericles*, ch. 9.

12 Plato, *Protagoras*, 322c–d.

13 Racine's masterpiece is a finer work than the one it draws its inspiration from.

14 Oswald Spengler, *The Decline of the West*, trans. Charles Francis Atkinson, Allen & Unwin, London, 1926–28.

15 There is no contemporary evidence of such a naming, nor indeed of any distinction being made in fifth-century Athens between the two main statues of Athena on the Acropolis. The one housed in the Parthenon was referred to as 'Athena', 'the god', or 'Athena Polias'. 'Athena Parthenos' may have started as a nickname, to distinguish it from the ancient statue in the Erechtheion. On this whole issue, see Herington.

16 Plato, *Cratylus*, s. 407b.

17 On the image of humans binding themselves to the yoke of Necessity, see Williams. Williams focuses on Agamemnon reluctantly strapping himself to his fate (ch. 6).

18 Alan L. Boegehild, 'Group and Single Competitions at the Panathenaic', in Neils (ed.), *Worshipping Athena*, pp. 96–7.

19 This polarity is different from that famously postulated by Nietzsche — the dualism of Dionysus and Apollo. Nietzsche's Dionysian principle represents barbaric, drunken instinct and violence — a Hobbesean underpinning of human existence in tooth and claw. It assumes that in all humans, just beneath the surface, there is an animal essence. One and all are governed by driving egoism and a relentless will to power. The true inner person is the satyr — half man, half devil-goat — a creature that inhabits the dark and primeval woods, a bubbling, unrepressed dynamo of lust and sadism. What the Erechtheion symbolises is different from Nietzsche's Dionysus. It is as if the Dionysian core is taken as a given; it is pre-cultural. The Karyatids are not satyrs, not brute stupid. They represent culture at its deepest — primal culture.

The Dionysian is countered by the Apollonian principle. Nietzsche identifies the god Apollo with veils of appearance, the misty dreams or illusions that mortals need to distract them from the Dionysian horrors of existence. Apollo represents culture — art and story, civilisation and order. He supplies redeeming illusions to make human life bearable· My counterpart to Nietzsche's Apollonian is the sun-drenched shining of the Parthenon. Yet it, too, is different. Apollonian culture is a sequence of consoling and inspiring, redemptive illusions. The Parthenon is not so ephemeral.

20 Hale, ch. 1.

21 Alfred North Whitehead, *Process and Reality*, Free Press, New York, 1979, p. 39.

22 Nietzsche, *The Birth of Tragedy*, pp. 135, 84, 91, 95.

23 Plato, *The Laws*, Book I, 647 a–d; Book II, 653 and 659; and Book V, 729 B.

24 'Eurhythmy' was singled out by the founder of the modern Olympics, Baron Pierre de Coubertin, as central to the pagan religious ideal embodied in the ancient Games. I shall take the concept up again in later chapters.

25 Rhodes, p. 36.

26 Philip Slater explores this at length, ch. XI.

27 Notably in the archaic period between the eighth and fifth centuries (Wilk, p. 31).

28 Susan Deacy, 'Athena and the Amazons', included in Alan B. Lloyd (ed.), *What is a God?*, pp. 155–7.

29 Deacy, op. cit., p. 158.

30 This is picked up and worked with masterful subtlety by Mark in his Life of Jesus, in his depiction of Peter — whose name Petros is given to him by Jesus, and means 'stone'. See my *The Existential Jesus*, especially chs. 1 & 7.

31 Aeschylus, *Eumenides*, *The Oresteia*, lines 854–5, 1023.

32 Aeschylus, *Agamemnon*, *The Oresteia*, lines 463–66.

33 Aristophanes staged his comedy, *The Clouds*, in 423 BC in Athens, two years before the Erechtheion was commenced. It mercilessly satirises Socrates. It is possible that the men who sculpted the Karyatids had a negative image of Socrates, cued by Aristophanes, somewhere in their minds — an image of the unworldliness of abstract philosophy and the airy superficiality of Reason.

34 *Agamemnon*, line 1149.

35 Raphael's *Transfiguration* gives rich pictorial representation to this chaos and its transcendence.

3. Delphi

1 Nietzsche, *The Birth of Tragedy*, section 9.

2 Maass, p. 99.

3 Gregory Nagy, 'The Name of Apollo', included in Solomon, pp. 6–7.

4 Schadewaldt, pp. 19–20.

5 Jenny Strauss Clay, 'Tendenz and Olympian Propaganda', included in Solomon, p. 34.

6 Clay, p. 36.

7 Plutarch, 'The E at Delphi', *Moralia*, vol. V, pp. 207–9.

8 Babbitt, ibid., p. 195.

9 Plutarch, pp. 201, 238–53. And, Roux, p. 216.

There is a marked parallel in Mark and John's Life of Jesus — both express the central teaching in the words *egō eimi*, 'I am'.

10 Some Poussin scholars, led by Anthony Blunt, have made the association with the Delphic E (Anthony Blunt, *Nicolas Poussin*, Pantheon, New York, 1967, pp. 195–205). Alain Mérot is one, although he interprets the epsilon as signalling 'eternity' (*Nicolas Poussin*, Thames & Hudson, London, 1990, p. 97). Richard Verdi takes Plutarch's 'you are' to refer to Peter, 'You are the one who will build my church' (*Nicolas Poussin*, Zwemmer, London, 1995, p. 251). Blunt rejected that possibility, seeing the E as a more general allusion, and also a possible linking of the Sacraments with the mysteries of Greek religion.

For reading John's Life of Jesus as centred on the 'I am', see Carroll, *The Existential Jesus*.

11 Maass, p. 8.

12 My main source is Georges Roux (pp. 64–70, 92–4).

13 E.g. Fontenrose, pp. 224–5.

14 Roux, pp. 98–100.

15 Burkert, p. 224.

16 Fontenrose, pp. 224–5.

17 Roux, p. 157.

18 Fontenrose, ch. 1.

19 Graves, p. 372.

20 Jean-Dominique Ingres, *Oedipe explique l'énigme du Sphinx*, 1808, Louvre. This painting brilliantly works Oedipal psychological themes, ninety years before Freud.

21 Maass, p. 218.

22 Petsas, pp.115–18.

23 Donald G. Kyle, 'Gifts and Glory', in Neils (ed.), *Worshipping Athena*, p. 117.

4. Homer

1 Walter Otto, p. 9.

2 For example, Homer, *Iliad*, trans. Lattimore, p. 29.

3 Burkert, p. 47.

4 Pausanias, 6. 23. 3.

5 Shakespeare, *Macbeth*, V, v, 26–8.

6 Book 5, lines 87–94.

7 Book 19, lines 282–300.

8 Book 24, lines 761–75.

9 Book 16, lines 739–50.

10 Book 6, lines 447–65.

11 Book 20, lines 498–503.

12 Mackie, pp. 41–6.

13 Book 21, lines 106–112.

14 Nagy, p. 62.
15 Walter Burkert sees Achilles as, in part, a double of Apollo — they have the same look (p. 147). Mackie notes their shared links with devastation, healing, and music (p. 147).
16 Nagy, ch. 5.
17 *Iliad* 9: 185–91.
18 Aeschylus, *Agamemnon*, l. 467–72.
19 Calasso, p. 387.
20 See Bernard Williams, ch. VI.
21 Jenny Strauss Clay (*The Wrath of Athena*) puts the strongest case that I have read for the complementarity of the two Epics, and their single authorship (see especially her Appendix).
22 Book XXIII, lines 314–15, Fitzgerald translation.
23 Clay, pp. 96–112.
24 Gregory Nagy, focusing more narrowly on the song of Demodokos, also reads it as a contest between *biē* and *mētis* — he suggests there are already hints in the *Iliad* of enmity between Achilles and Odysseus (ch. 4 and p. 62).
25 *Odyssey*, Book XIII, l. 371–7.
26 Griffin, p. 168.
27 Christopher Hibbert, *Wellington*, HarperCollins, London, 1997, p. 142.
28 Victor Davis Hanson, *Why the West has Won*, Faber and Faber, London, 2002, ch. 3; quote from p. 63.
29 Hanson, p. 71.
30 Hanson, p. 79.
31 Hammond, pp. 123–5.
32 Renault, pp. 44–5. Renault's biography is pitched at the eulogistic extreme.

On Achilles the healer , see *Iliad* 11: 825–31.
33 Renault, pp. 66–70.
34 For example, Michael Wood, pp. 114–115.
35 Plutarch, *The Lives*, p. 551.
36 Wood, p. 71.
37 Hanson goes so far as to liken Alexander to Hitler — both were, in his words, 'half-educated pop philosophers who sprinkled their orders of mass destruction with allusions to literature and poetry' (pp. 89–90). This summing up is indicative of the intensity of feeling that Alexander arouses, leading to biographies that range in their extremity from the rhapsodic to the demonic.

5. Athena

1 Burkert argues that the goddess was named after the city (p. 139). Karl Kerenyi (*Athene*) and Otto (p. 46) put the opposite case, that the city was named after Athena.

I have found Walter Otto's book the most useful background

reflection for parts of this chapter. Otto's title in the original German is *Die Götter Griechenlands: Das Bild des Göttlichen im Spiegel des griechischen Geistes*. The English, *The Homeric Gods*, is a rather bland, narrowing translation of *The Greek Gods: the Image of the Divine in the Mirror of the Greek Mind*.

2 Otto, p. 3.

3 *Agamemnon*, l. 160.

4 Herington, p. 56. I am indebted to Herington generally in this discussion, especially his ch. VII.

5 Donald Kagan, *Pericles of Athens and the Birth of Democracy*.

6 Thucydides, p. 119.

7 Kagan, p. 146.

8 Alan L. Boegehold, 'Group and Single Competition at the Panathenaia', in Jennifer Neils (ed.), *Worshipping Athena*, pp. 96–8.

9 Kasper–Butz, p. 167.

10 Otto, p. 9.

11 Kerenyi, *Gods of the Greeks*, pp. 118–21. Otto persuasively combats the view of some scholars that this myth is a late post–Homeric invention (pp. 50–52).

12 Graves, p. 96; Otto, p. 45.

13 Kasper–Butz, p. 181.

14 Kerenyi, *Gods of the Greeks*, p. 128.

15 Neils, *Goddess and Polis*, pp. 103–117.

16 Otto, pp. 53–60.

17 *Iliad*, 10, 278–9.

18 Shearer, p. 26.

19 Pindar, p. 47.

20 *lliad*, 8, 373.

21 Henry George Liddell and Robert Scott, *A Greek–English Lexicon*, 9th edition, Oxford University Press, Oxford, 1996.

22 For example, the 360 BC head of Hygeia (one of the aliases for Athena), probably from the Temple of Athena Alea in Tegea, housed in the National Archaeological Museum in Athens (see p 116).

23 Otto, p. 161.

24 This metaphor is borrowed from Nietzsche, who praises the philosopher with a tuning fork, sounding the values of the time to hear how hollow they sound (*Twilight of the Idols*).

25 I have developed this view — of the composite *I* — at length in my *The Existential Jesus* (ch. 6).

26 Herodotus, I.91.

27 Lattimore translation. 'Muse' appears in the first line of the *Odyssey*, 'goddess, daughter of Zeus' in the tenth.

28 I have reflected on this at greater length in my *The Western Dreaming*, ch. 1.

29 For example, Henry James' Preface to *Portrait of a Lady*.

6. The Heritage

1 The chronology is rough — for one, Homer may have lived earlier in the eighth century. The first Olympic Games were held in 776 BC, with one event, a foot race. In 724 BC other races were added, and in 708 BC a range of events. Then, in the early seventh century, the site was developed, including the first temples.

2 The theme of cheerfulness appears in different parts of *The Birth of Tragedy*, and that of gratitude in *Beyond Good and Evil*.

3 I reflect on this at length in *The Existential Jesus*.

4 More precisely, it is the second key turning point. Nietzsche located the first, identifying it with Socrates, and the shift he engineered away from *mythos*, and into centring human value and meaning on a rationalist ethics (*The Birth of Tragedy*). This shift is from Homer to a moralist intellectualism.

5 This is a quite specific criticism of Christianity, limited to the domain of metaphysical history. It does not imply support, or sympathy for a broader anti-Christian perspective. This is not the place to chart the positive role of the churches in the history of the West, but such a charting would include the following: promulgating and sanctioning a moral code regulating everyday life, making it more civil and decent; reinforcing community; encouraging public responsibility; preserving manuscripts, and traditions of learning, especially through the dark thousand years following the collapse of the Roman Empire; developing a tradition of biblical scholarship and theology that would feed into a broad range of secular academic disciplines; patronising much of the great art of the Renaissance; and, in a general sense, playing a major role in the development of Western civilisation.

6 I have examined this at length in a study of the metaphysical failure of Humanism in *The Wreck of Western Culture*.

7 John 3: 8.

8 Raphael's greatest paintings of the Madonna and Child, led by the Sistine Madonna, are explicitly Christian. Yet, they portray the tragic destiny of a mother who can foresee what is going to befall her baby son. As such, Raphael's Madonnas are reminiscent of Kassandra.

9 *Iliad*, 11, 305–309.

10 *Iliad*, 20, 164–74.

11 The one source I have drawn on for the Kassandra story is Aeschylus' *Agamemnon*.

12 The Parthenon was built on roughly the same site as the older Parthenon destroyed by the Persians in 480 BC, although it was larger, and positioned more to the west and to the north (Hurwit, *The Acropolis in the Age of Pericles*, p. 116). Continuity may have been the main reason for this siting, but earlier temples had been positioned over towards the north side of the Acropolis, near the Erechtheion. No doubt, a number of considerations influenced Perikles on the siting of the Parthenon; visibility from the Pnyx may have been one of them.

BIBLIOGRAPHY

Aeschylus, *Agamemnon*, edited with introduction and commentary by J. D. Denniston and D. L. Page, Oxford University Press, Oxford, 1957

Aeschylus, *Oresteia*, trans. Richmond Lattimore, University of Chicago Press, Chicago, 1953

Aristophanes, *Five Comedies*, trans, Benjamin Bickley Rogers, Doubleday, New York, 1955

Aristotle, *Nicomachean Ethics,* Loeb Classical Library, Harvard University Press, Cambridge, Mass., 1934

Aristotle, *Poetics*, trans. S. H. Butcher, Constable, London, 1951

Boardman, John, *Greek Sculpture: the Archaic Period*, Thames and Hudson, London, 1978

Boardman, John, *The Parthenon and its Sculptures,* Thames and Hudson, London, 1985

Bremmer, Jan N., *The Early Greek Concept of the Soul*, Princeton University Press, Princeton, 1987

Burkert, Walter, *Greek Religion*, trans. John Raffan, Blackwell, Oxford, 1985

Calasso, Roberto, *The Marriage of Cadmus and Harmony*, trans. Tim Parks, Knopf, New York, 1993

Carroll, John, *The Existential Jesus*, Scribe, Melbourne, 2007

Carroll, John, *The Western Dreaming*, HarperCollins, Sydney, 2001

Carroll, John, *The Wreck of Western Culture: humanism revisited*, Scribe, Melbourne, 2004

Clay, Jenny Strauss, *The Wrath of Athena*, Princeton University Press, Princeton, 1983

Dodds, E. R., *The Greeks and the Irrational*, University of California Press, Berkeley, 1951

Euripides, 5 volumes included in *The Complete Greek Tragedies*, University of Chicago Press, Chicago, 1955–9

Fontenrose, Joseph, *The Delphic Oracle*, University of California Press, Berkeley, 1978

Goette, Hans R., *Athens, Attica, and the Megarid: an archaeological guide*, Routledge, London, 2001

Griffin, Jasper, *Homer on Life and Death*, Oxford University Press, Oxford, 1980

Hale, John R., *Lords of the Sea: the epic story of the Athenian navy and the birth of democracy*, Penguin, London, 2009

Hammond, N. G. L., *Alexander the Great*, Noyes Press, New Jersey, 1980

Herington, C. J., *Athena Parthenos and Athena Polias*, Manchester University Press, Manchester, 1955

Herodotus, *The Histories*, trans. Aubrey de Selincourt, Penguin, London, 1972

Homer, *The Iliad*, Loeb Classical Library, Harvard University Press, Cambridge, Mass., 1924

Homer, *The Iliad*, trans. Richmond Lattimore, University of Chicago Press, Chicago, 1951

Homer, *The Odyssey*, trans. Robert Fitzgerald, Heinemann, London, 1961

Homer, *The Odyssey*, trans. Richmond Lattimore, Harper & Row, New York, 1967

Hurwit, Jeffrey M., *The Acropolis in the Age of Pericles*, Cambridge University Press, Cambridge, 2004

Hurwit, Jeffrey M., *The Athenian Acropolis*, Cambridge University Press, Cambridge, 1999

Kagan, Donald, *Pericles of Athens and the Birth of Democracy*, Secker & Warburg, London, 1990

Kasper–Butz, Irmgard, *Die Göttin Athena im klassischen Athen*, Peter Lang, Frankfurt-am-Main, 1990

Kerenyi, Karl, *Athene: Virgin and Mother*, trans. Murray Stein, Spring, Zurich, 1978

Kerenyi, Karl, *The Gods of the Greeks*, Thames & Hudson, London, 1951

Lloyd, Alan B. (ed.), *What is a God?*, Duckworth, London, 1997

Maass, Michael, *Das Antike Delphi*, Wissenschaftliche Buchgesellschaft, Darmstadt, 1993

Mackie, C. J., *Rivers of Fire: mythic themes in Homer's Iliad*, New Academia Publishing, Washington DC, 2008

Nagy, Gregory, *The Best of the Achaeans*, Johns Hopkins University Press, Baltimore, 1979

Neils, Jenifer, *Goddess and Polis*, Princeton University Press, Princeton, 1992

Neils, Jenifer, (ed.), *Worshipping Athena*, University of Wisconsin Press, 1996

Nietzsche, Friedrich, *The Birth of Tragedy*, included in *Basic Writings of Nietzsche*, ed. and trans. Walter Kaufmann, Modern Library, New York, 1968

Nietzsche, Friedrich, *Die Geburt der Tragödie*, Reclam, Stuttgart, 1981

Otto, Walter F., *The Homeric Gods*, trans. Moses Hadas, Thames & Hudson, 1979

Paton, J. M. (ed.), *The Erechtheon*, Cambridge, Mass., 1927

Pausanias, *Guide to Greece*, trans. Peter Levi, Penguin, 1979

Petsas, Photios, *Delphi*, Krene Editions, Athens, 2004

Pindar, *The Odes*, trans. C. M. Bowra, Penguin, London, 1969

Plato, *The Collected Dialogues of Plato*, ed. Edith Hamilton and Huntington Cairns, Princenton University Press, Princeton, 1963

Plutarch, *The Lives*, University of Chicago, Chicago, 1952

Plutarch, *Moralia*, vol. V, with trans. by Frank Cole Babbitt, Harvard University Press, London, 1957

Renault, Mary, *The Nature of Alexander*, Penguin, London, 2001

Rhodes, Robin Francis, *Architecture and Meaning on the Athenian Acropolis*, Cambridge University Press, Cambridge, 1995

Roux, Georges, *Delphes: son oracle et ses dieux*, Société d'Éditions 'Les Belles Lettres', Paris, 1976

Ruprecht, Louis A., *Was Greek Thought Religious?*, Palgrave, New York, 2002

Schadewaldt, Wolfgang, *Der Gott von Delphi und die Humanitätsidee*, Neske, Pfullingen, 1965

Shearer, Ann, *Athena: image and energy*, Viking Arkana, London, 1996

Slater, Philip, *The Glory of Hera*, Beacon Press, Boston, 1968

Slattery, Luke, *Dating Aphrodite*, ABC Books, Sydney 2005

Solomon, Jon, ed., *Apollo: origins and influences*, University of Arizona Press, Tucson, 1994

Sophocles, *Oedipus the King*, trans, David Grene, included in *The Complete Greek Tragedies*, Sophocles I, University of Chicago Press, 1954

Spatheri, Elsie, *Mycenae*, Hesperos, Athens, 2004

Thucydides, *History of the Peloponnesian War*, trans. Rex Warner, Penguin, London, 1954

Wilk, Stephen R., *Medusa*, Oxford University Press, Oxford, 2000

Williams, Bernard, *Shame and Necessity*, University of California Press, Berkeley, 1993

Wood, Michael, *In the Footsteps of Alexander the Great*, BBC Books, London, 1997

GLOSSARY OF PEOPLE AND PLACES

- Achilles, son of Peleus and the goddess Thetis, warrior hero, principal character in the *Iliad*
- Acropolis in Athens, rock citadel on which the Parthenon stands
- Adyton, small chamber at the rear of the Temple of Apollo in Delphi in which the Oracle sat
- Aegis, shield of Athena, with the Medusa head at its centre
- Aeschylus, 525–456 BC, soldier and dramatist, author of *Agamemnon*
- Agamemnon, c 1200 BC, king of Mycenae, leader of the Greeks in the Trojan War
- *Agamemnon*, 458 BC, first play in the *Oresteian Trilogy*, by Aeschylus
- Alexander the Great, 356–323 BC, Macedonian, conqueror and civiliser
- Amazons, legendary tribe of warrior women, defeated by Theseus
- Anaxagoras, c 500–428 BC, philosopher

- Andromache, wife of Hektor
- Aphrodite (Roman goddess Venus), goddess of beauty and erotic love
- Apollo, son of Zeus, twin brother of Artemis, sun god, associated with archery, music, and prophecy
- Arachne, maiden turned into a spider by Athena, for challenging her artistry at weaving
- Arcadia, mountainous region of Greece situated in the central Peloponnese, fabled as an earthly paradise
- Ares, god of war
- Aristides the Just, 530–468 BC, Athenian political leader
- Aristophanes, 448–385 BC, comic dramatist in Athens
- Aristotle, 384–322 BC, philosopher
- Artemis (Roman goddess Diana), moon goddess, associated with chastity, the hunt, and caring for the earth and wildlife
- Aspasia of Miletus, de-facto wife of Perikles
- Athena, daughter of Zeus, goddess of wisdom
- Athena Parthenos, 10-metre high statue carved by Pheidias, housed in the Parthenon
- Athena Polias, ancient olivewood statue, housed in the Erechtheion
- Attika, small region of Greece that includes Athens
- Briseis, slave mistress of Achilles
- Chronos, father of Zeus
- Croesus of Lydia, 595–c 547 BC, richest man in the world
- Cyclades, circle of islands in the middle of the Aegean Sea with Delos at the centre
- *Daimon, daimonia*, spirit forces, demi-gods
- Darius the Great, 522–486 BC, Persian king who invaded Greece in 490 BC, defeated by the Athenians at Macedon

- Darius III, Persian king, defeated by Alexander the Great at Gaugamela in 331 BC
- Delos, small island in the Aegean Sea, birthplace of Apollo and Artemis, site of the panhellenic sanctuary of Apollo
- Delphi, small town in Phokis, on the side of Mt Parnassos, home of the Delphic Oracle
- Delphi Charioteer, 474 BC, bronze statue
- Demodokos, blind minstrel at the Phaiakian court in the *Odyssey*
- Diomedes, son of Tydeus, one of the leading Greek warriors at Troy
- Dionysus (or Bacchus), god of wine and revelry
- Diotima, prophetess who taught Socrates everything he knew about love
- Doric, early order of Greek architecture, characterised by plain columns (without bases) and plain capitals
- Eleusis, small town close to Athens, site of sanctuary of Artemis
- Entablature, the upper elements of a temple supported by the columns
- Erechtheion, temple on the Athenian Acropolis, built 421–406 BC
- Erechthonius, perhaps first king of Athens, raised by Athena
- Euripides, 484–407 BC, tragic dramatist
- Fates (*moirai*), three beautiful women who spin the fate of each mortal
- Gaia, goddess of the earth
- Gaugamela, site of Alexander the Great's final and decisive battle against the Persians, in 331 BC
- *Glaux*, small owl found in Athens
- Gorgons, three monstrous sisters with snakes for hair and a transfixing gaze

- Hektor, son of Priam, preeminent Trojan warrior
- Helen, wife of Menelaus, renowned beauty who absconds with Paris to Troy
- Helios, sun god
- Hephaestion, c 356–324 BC, Macedonian general and bosom friend of Alexander the Great
- Hephaistos, god, son of Zeus, blacksmith to the gods
- Hera, goddess, wife of Zeus
- Herakles, mythical hero and god, strongman, famous for his twelve labours
- Hesiod, c 750–700 BC, author of the *Theogony* and *Works and Days*
- Hippolytus, son of Theseus, character in Euripides' tragedy *Hippolytus*
- Homer, c 750–700 BC, poet, author of the *Iliad* and the *Odyssey*
- *Iliad*, c 700 BC, epic poem composed by Homer
- Ionic, order of Greek architecture, following the Doric, with more ornate capitals to the columns
- Jokasta, mother and wife of Oedipus
- Karyatids, c 420 BC, six statues of maidens forming columns that support the roof of the south portico of the Erechtheion
- Kassandra, Trojan princess, daughter of King Priam, given the gift of prophecy by Apollo, enslaved by Agamemnon, killed by Klytemnestra
- Kastalian spring, source of sacred water for purification in Delphi
- Kimon, 510–450 BC, Athenian naval commander and political leader
- Klytemnestra, Queen of Mycenae, wife of Agamemnon
- Laius, king of Thebes, father of Oedipus
- Lykaon, son of Priam, killed by Achilles

- Marathon, 42 kilometres from Athens, site of the battle in 490 BC at which the Athenians defeated a much larger army of Persians
- Medusa, one of the Gorgon sisters, killed by Perseus; her head adorns the shield of Athena
- Megaron, large central interior of a Greek temple
- Metis, mother of Athena, known for her wise counsel
- Miltiades, 550–489 BC, Athenian general who defeated the Persians at Marathon; political leader
- Mt Olympus, predominant mountain in northern Greece
- Mt Parnassus, sacred mountain on the north side of the Gulf of Corinth, north-west of Athens; Delphi is halfway up one of its sides
- Muses, goddesses patroning creative inspiration in the arts, followers of Apollo
- Mycenae, citadel in the Peloponnese, capital of the Mycenaean Empire, which ended c 1200 BC
- Necessity (*anagkē*), supernatural force, mother of the Fates
- Nike, goddess of victory
- Odysseus, king of Ithaca, Greek hero at Troy, principal character in Homer's *Odyssey*
- *Odyssey*, c 700 BC, Homer's second work
- Oedipus, mythical king of Thebes, who killed his father and married his mother
- Olympia, town in the Peloponnese, near Arcadia, site of the Olympic Games
- Omphalos, stone shaped like a giant acorn, symbolising Delphi as the navel of the earth
- *Oresteia*, 458 BC, tragic trilogy by Aeschylus
- Orphism, obscure Greek cult linked to the mythic figure of

Orpheus, the tragic minstrel

- Parmenion, c 400–330 BC, Macedonian general who fought under Alexander the Great
- Parthenon, temple to Athena, built in Athens 447–438 BC
- Patroklos, Greek warrior in the Trojan War, bosom friend of Achilles
- Pausanias, c 150 AD, Greek travel writer
- Pediment, the triangular space above the columns at the end of a temple
- Peleus, father of Achilles
- Peloponnesian War, 431–404 BC, fought between Athens and Sparta, won by the Spartans
- Penelope, wife of Odysseus
- Peplos, rectangular wool cloak woven annually to clothe Athena Polias
- Perikles, 490–429 BC, Athenian leader, creator of the Acropolis buildings
- Perseus, mythic figure, son of Zeus, killer of the Medusa
- Pheidias, sculptor, responsible for the overall conception of the Parthenon
- Philip II, 382–336 BC, King of Macedon, father of Alexander the Great
- Phokis, region of Greece, north–west of Attika, which includes Delphi
- Piraeus, the port of Athens
- Plato, 428–348 BC, philosopher
- Plutarch, 46–120 AD, Greek essayist and author of *Lives of Prominent Greeks and Romans*; priest of Apollo in Delphi
- Pnyx, site in Athens for public meetings, birthplace of democracy
- Polyphemos, one-eyed giant Cyclops, son of Poseidon

- Poseidon, god of the sea, brother of Zeus, associated with earthquakes and storms
- Priam, King of Troy
- Pronaos, foyer in a Greek temple
- Propylaia, marble buildings that lead onto the top of the Acropolis in Athens
- Protagoras, 481–411 BC, philosopher
- Pythian Games, held in Delphi every four years
- Pytho, Pythia, alternative name for the Delphic Oracle; also the giant snake that originally occupied Delphi, killed by Apollo
- Rhea, wife of Chronos, mother of Zeus
- Roxana, c 345–310 BC, Baktrian wife of Alexander the Great
- Salamis, island in the Saronic Gulf close to Athens, next to which the Athenian navy defeated a much larger Persian force in 480 BC
- Satyr, mythic creature, half human, half goat
- Silenus, mythic figure, follower of Dionysus; both debauched and wise
- Sirens, bird-like monsters in the *Odyssey* with the heads of women, who drew sailors to their death with their haunting singing
- Skamandros, river near Troy
- Socrates, 470–399 BC, philosopher
- Solon, c 638–558 BC, Athenian political leader, poet, and lawmaker
- Sophocles, c 495–406 BC, prominent Athenian citizen and tragic dramatist, author of *Oedipus the King*
- Sparta, city and region in the south of the Peloponnese, noted for its militarism
- Sphinx, mythic creature with demonic powers; the Theban

sphinx had a woman's head, a lioness's body, a serpent's tail, and eagle's wings

- Sphinx of Naxos, giant statue at Delphi
- Stoicism, school of philosophy, emphasising character, balance, and fortitude
- Teiresias, blind seer who tells Oedipus the truth about himself
- Telemachos, son of Odysseus
- Thebes, capital of Boeotia, site of the Theban cycle of tragedies
- Themistokles, 524–458 BC, Athenian naval commander who defeated the Persians at Salamis in 480 BC; political leader
- Theseus, mythic early king of Athens and hero
- Thucydides, 460–400 BC, Athenian citizen, author of the *History of the Peloponnesian War*
- Troy, city on the north-west corner of Asia Minor (modern Turkey)
- Vitruvius, c 80–15 BC, Roman architect
- Xenophon, c 430–354 BC, Athenian soldier and historian
- Xerxes, Persian king who invaded Greece in 480 BC, defeated in the naval battle of Salamis
- Zeus, king of the gods
- Zeus of Artemisium, c 460 BC, bronze statue of a javelin thrower

INDEX